Leadership on Trial:
Lessons from The Apprentice

Ann Vanino

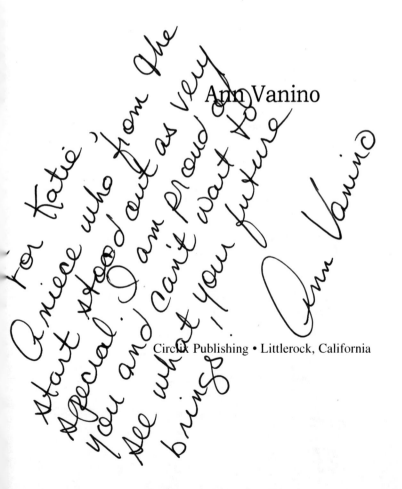

Circux Publishing • Littlerock, California

Published by

Circlix Publishing
P.O. Box 1372
Littlerock, CA 93543
(661) 944-6329

Book Design by Lisa Wysocky, White Horse Enterprises

First edition published January 2005

The Library of Congress Cataloging-in-Publication Data Applied For

Vanino, Ann, 1952 –
Leadership on Trial: Lessons from The Apprentice
Ann Vanino.—1st ed.
cm.
ISBN 978-0-9762281-0-3
1. Business   2. Self-Help   I. Title
2005

Copyright © 2005 by Ann Vanino

All rights reserved

Printed in the United States of America

1 3 5 7 9 10 8 6 4 2

No part of this book may be reproduced, stored in a retrieval system, or transmitted by any means, electronic, mechanical, photocopying, recording, or otherwise, without written permission from the author.

This book contains information of a general nature. The business world is ever changing and dynamic and involves risks and uncertainties. The author and publisher cannot and do not warrant or guarantee that use of information in this book will work for you. This book was not authorized, prepared, licensed, approved, or endorsed by any entity or person involved in creating, producing or participating in *The Apprentice* television series. This book and all advice, strategy and descriptions contained herein are the author's views and analysis and do not purport to be opinions of any other person or entity.

For information regarding special discounts for bulk purchases, please contact us at
Ann@MovingForward.net

This book is dedicated to
my husband, Ermanno Vanino
and
my teacher, Lynn Andrews

Thank you for all you are to me.

ACKNOWLEDGEMENTS

First, my thanks to Shane Bowlin, virtual assistant extraordinaire, who came the whole way with me on this book. Your knowledge of the book publishing world, insights, guidance, friendship, and support mean the world to me. My husband and business partner, Ermanno Vanino, gave me the idea to write this book and believed in it all the way. Thank you to my family, Jane and Jim Burner, Robert and Melani Dizard, Mary and Tom Homan, Frank and Robyn Vignuli, Gerard and Lisa Vignuli and your wonderful families for your support. My nephew, Robert Homan and his parents, Tom and Mary provided encouragement and many contributions to the book. To my extended family, Ida and Jerry Orr, Julie and Hector Arencibia, Mark Orr and Heather Edwards, Anna and Roger Kleckner, and Cheryl and Eric Ramberger, thank you for your support and for being in my life. Thank you to my aunt and uncle, Wilson and Lynn Wood Dizard for your encouragement of my writing and for being role models throughout my life to set my sights high. My parents, Robert and Charlotte Cullen Dizard have passed on, but their love for me and belief in me continue to guide my way.

My teacher, Lynn Andrews and my circle within The Lynn Andrews Center for Sacred Arts and Training and its Continuing Education Program have been so important in this journey. Special thanks to the Star Woman Lodge for your support and enthusiasm for this book. Thank you to Lillian Smith, who has mentored and guided my writing and started it all by asking me to write a coaching column for her paper, *The Agua Dulce/Acton Country Journal*. Special thanks to my professor and mentor Lou Ismay for all you have given me. Thank you to The Coaches Training Institute for your excellent coach training and for giving me the foundation I needed to succeed. Several coaches have given me invaluable support along the way. Leslie Lupinsky was my first coach and gave me my start. Deb Traverso's excellent coaching got me going in the world of writing and publishing. Thank you to Kat Kehres for your branding and business planning coaching. You all make such a difference. Thank you too to Cheryl Richardson and Laura Berman-Fortgang. You are pioneer coaches. Your books and seminars guided my way as I began my coaching and continue to do so. Thank you too to The International Coach Federation for leading the coaching profession worldwide. Thank you to Professor Dennis Smith of New York University's Wagner Graduate School of Public Service for your help with my efforts. I am proud to be a Wagner alumnus. Thank you to Shane's client circle, particularly authors Beth Mende-Conny, Deb Traverso, and Lynn Robinson, for supporting me and letting me watch as you walked the path ahead of me. Now I have a book and walk a little closer.

Many friends have supported me in the writing of this book. Susan Rethy gave so much enthusiasm as I began this project. Her keen insights brought me further in my analysis of the leadership lessons of the show. Thank you to Daniel Castro for being there from the start and ready to support this book in any way. As I wrote the book, many friends contributed to it and supported me including, Karen Erstad, Diana Peterson-More, Veronica Wirth, Joanne Slaboch, Jane Stenehjem, Heather Rem, Kristine Dale, Mary Catherine Fish, Susan Cranston, Kirsten Hermann, Barb Keller, Christine Prout, Jillian Alexander-Gregory, Joanne May, Michelle Gardner, Scarlet Rivera, Sally Kraus, Marcia Williams, Juanita Grundmann, Suzanne Young, Linda Boyle and Debra Crouch.

In putting this book together the expertise of Lisa Wysocky, for editing and layout; and David Gurnick and Tal Grinblat of Lewitt, Hackman, Shapiro, Marshall, and Harlan were invaluable. Finally, thank you to Donald Trump, Mark Burnett, and the candidates on the first season of *The Apprentice* for an intelligent show that gives us many good lessons as we navigate the business world.

TABLE OF CONTENTS

Introduction		1
Chapter One	"You're Fired!" Views on Leadership	9
Chapter Two	Lesson One: Take Risks "Would I do it again? Absolutely!" —Heidi Bressler	13
Chapter Three	Lesson Two: Be Yourself "I made it, Mama!" —Troy McClain	37
Chapter Four	Lesson Three: Know the Game "IQ may not be the greatest factor in selling lemonade." —David Gould	59
Chapter Five	Lesson Four: Maintain Balance "Heidi, do you need to leave?" —Donald Trump	81
Chapter Six	Lesson Five: Have a Strategy "I am a good person who knows how to fight for what she believes in." —Omarosa Manigault-Stallworth	105
Chapter Seven	Lesson Six: Think Outside the Box "Protégé did not think outside the box and took a severe thumping." —Donald Trump	127
Chapter Eight	Lesson Seven: Know When to Join and When to Lead "All I said was I think we were duped." —Tammy Lee	149
Chapter Nine	"You're Hired!" Winning "Now that I've been fired, I realize he was saying, 'Win this, Sam.'" —Sam Solovey	169
Appendix A	A Guide to Viewing *The Apprentice* as a Case Study	179
Appendix B	Leadership Resources	183

INTRODUCTION

My life has been a journey to understanding personal power. I have watched leaders with great intensity. The best leaders are those who understand power and people. They use this knowledge to make the world a better place. Leaders guide, mentor, organize, inspire, and lead. When I first entered the work force, I was fascinated with how people interact. I watched managers disregard people for products, manage by fear, and not get too far in the process. I watched managers who did not understand people or themselves. I also watched managers who understood both power and people—they gave the people they managed motivation and guidance. They understood how people interact, what they need, and what gets people working together. They understood power—how it works, how people use it, and how to access it within. This combination of understanding power and people is a hallmark of true leadership.

Through my career, I have led and been led. As I rose to higher positions in government and business, I found myself stumbling at times. I continued succeeding, but began to realize that my leadership skills needed a stronger foundation. I needed to understand power—and myself—better. As I recognized this, a teacher appeared. Her name is Lynn Andrews. She is a leader in the field of personal development and spirituality. At first, I thought that working with Lynn would take me to a mountaintop in Tibet (literally!). But instead we went to the heart of me. Her guidance helped me understand what true power is. She helped me see practical, engaging, and timeless truths that guide true leaders. I began to understand what leadership is.

In 1996, I became a personal and professional coach. My specialty is working with people to find fulfillment in their work. Now I see the journey in a kaleidoscope of ways. All my work returns to the same place: understanding power and people will help you be an effective leader.

The Apprentice

There is no question that *The Apprentice* is a wildly successful show. Forty million viewers tuned in to the first season. Why such popularity? The show is a primer on leadership—every episode is a business case study. Viewers see what works, what doesn't and why. The show sets up a competition among bright and accomplished individuals from whom we can learn. We get a glimpse of Donald Trump's world and how he thinks about success in business. Each episode offers lessons in winning and losing. We see the personal side of the candidates as they live together in close quarters and respond to the events of each day. The show gives viewers a benchmark against which to assess their own performance in the work world. Ultimately, *The Apprentice* succeeds because everyone wants to win.

Initially, I had not intended to watch *The Apprentice*. It wasn't for any particular reason. I was busy and it was not on my radar. Then, on the morning of January 4, 2004 I opened the *New York Times* to find a review of the show. The review said the show was about power, how to pursue it and achieve it. I was intrigued and watched the first episode. I was hooked. From the start, the show offered many lessons on leadership. Viewers have before them a glimpse of what Donald Trump is looking for, the tests of leadership that one faces in business, and winning and losing. Donald Trump wants a leader. I looked forward to each episode and became engrossed in the leadership lessons of the show. My interest led me to write this book.

The Book

This book is based on the first season of *The Apprentice*. From that season, I culled seven lessons on leadership. Chapter One sets the stage for these lessons by offering my views on leadership, using the show as a guide. Chapters Two through Eight present the seven lessons. Each of these chapters first explains the lesson in the context of *The Apprentice*. Then the chapter turns to an in depth look at the lesson in the context of understanding power and people. Chapter Nine looks at what *The Apprentice* teaches us about winning and helps you define what winning means to you. Appendix A suggests that you view each episode of the show as a business case study and offers ways to do just that. This will enhance your ability to cull the leadership lessons from the show. Appendix B offers resources available to you to further explore the seven leadership lessons.

Throughout the book, I refer to the cast of the show frequently. Following is a brief guide to the people who comprised the cast of *The Apprentice*.

Donald Trump
Born and raised in New York City
Graduate of the Wharton School of Finance
Stars in the NBC reality show *The Apprentice*
Billionaire real estate developer
Best-selling author, public speaker, philanthropist
Owns part of the three largest beauty competitions in the world

Carolyn Kepcher
Executive Vice President of the Trump Organization
Chief Operating Officer and General Manager for the Trump National
    Golf Clubs New York and New Jersey
Has been with the Trump Organization since 1994
Boardroom judge on *The Apprentice*

George H. Ross
Executive Vice President/Senior Counsel for the Trump organization
Business and legal advisor to Donald J. Trump
Has been with the organization since 1996
Adjunct professor at the New York University School of Professional Studies and Continuing Education
Boardroom judge on *The Apprentice*

Bill Rancic
The winner of *The Apprentice* (first season)
Founded CigarsAroundTheWorld.com with very little money— now it's a multi-million dollar national operation
Corporate spokesperson for Advanta Corp.
Real Estate developer, public speaker, author
Bachelor of Science degree from Loyola University
Resides in Lincoln Park, Illinois

Kwame Jackson
Born in Washington, D.C.; raised in Charlotte, North Carolina
B.S. in Business Administration from the University of North Carolina at Chapel Hill (Awarded HBS John F. Lebor "Entrepreneurial/New Ventures" Fellowship)
M.B.A. from Harvard (Awarded Kenan-Flagler Business School Leadership Excellence Award)
Fortune 500 experience: sales and marketing roles at Procter & Gamble and on Wall Street as an investment manager for Goldman Sachs
Founded a real estate development and investment company—Legacy Development Partners LLC, in 2004

Amy Henry
Raised in Arlington, Texas; lives in Austin, Texas
Graduated Magna Cum Laude from Texas A&M University

M.B.A. from Texas Christian University (Neeley Scholar, graduated in the top of her class)
Career: seven years working for leading U.S. technology companies
Had millions in stock options but lost heavily in the dot.com bust
Volunteer for non-profit GENAustin in Austin, Texas

Katrina Campins
Born and raised in Miami, Florida; currently resides in Coral Gables, Florida
B.B.A. in International Finance and Marketing from the University of Miami (4.0 G.P.A)
Licensed Florida Real Estate Agent who specializes in an elite clientele (executives, sports figures, diplomats and celebrities)
Ranks in top 3 percent of all Realtors nationwide
Weekly correspondent for ESPN and special assignments for CNBC
Host of South Florida real estate show

Heidi Bressler
Raised in Wayne, New Jersey; currently resides in Philadelphia
Undergraduate degree from Ithaca College
Master's in Criminology from American University (graduated in top of class)
Worked with former F.B.I. and secret service agents at the National Center for Missing and Exploited Children and as senior account executive at Qwest Communications

Omarosa Manigault-Stallworth
Raised in the projects of Youngstown, Ohio
Former political appointee in the Clinton and Gore White House
Currently a political consultant in Washington, D.C.
Graduated from Central State University
Master's degree from Howard University
Working toward Ph.D.
Volunteer at Maya Angelou Public Charter School

Nick Warnock

Raised in Bayonne, New Jersey; resides in Los Angeles, California
A star athlete much of his youth; played football at collegiate level
Attended the University of Richmond for a brief time; degree in English Literature from the University of San Diego
Launched a small Italian ice business, Nick's Authentic Italian Ice, during summer while in college
Headed a sales team for Xerox in Los Angeles, California

Troy McClain

Born in Anchorage, Alaska; raised in Alaska and Montana; currently resides in Boise, Idaho
Owned a party promotion company, a t-shirt company, and a health club
Lender, mortgage broker, benefits consultant, and real estate investor
Involved in real estate development and owns seven properties
Took on responsibility of supporting his mother and sister and was unable to pursue a higher education
Started boxing program at Morning Star Boys Ranch near Spokane
Co-founded Solution Source Media which offers solutions and products related to credit and real estate
Spokesperson for Pinnacle Financial Corporation
Resides in Boise, Idaho with his wife Crystal

Ereka Vetrini

Native New Yorker
Graduated with honors from Boston College
Worked in Hong Kong, Australia, Greece and Spain as an internal operations consultant for Estee Lauder
Worked as a global promotional marketing manager for Clinique
Growing up she learned her business principles by working in her parent's pizzeria
Announcer and sidekick for Tony Danza's daytime talk show

Tammy Lee
Asian-American stockbroker
B.A. in Economics from the University of Washington
TV commercial acting and stockbroker for Merrill Lynch's private client group (was assistant vice president when she left there in 2002)
Lives in Seattle, Washington

Bowie Hogg
Born and raised in Dallas, Texas
Attended United States Military Academy Preparatory School
Business degree from Texas A&M University.
Worked as an account executive at FedEx handling multi-million dollar accounts
Currently a motivational speaker and life coach

Sam Solovey
Raised in suburbs of Washington, D.C; resides in Chevy Chase, Maryland
Graduated from Colgate University
Worked for Accenture (formerly Andersen Consulting) in New York City and Washington, D.C. as change management analyst
Hosted radio talk show, *The Untrained Psychologist*
In 1999, co-founded *Potomac Tech Wire*, a tech newsletter
Director of Business Operations and Customer Relations for the entire family of Tech Wire publications
Founded Solovey's, an auctioneering business for charities and corporate fundraisers

Jessie Conners
Born in Minnesota; grew up traveling from Minneapolis to a two-hundred-sixty-five acre farm in Wisconsin with no running water or electricity to an orphanage in Monterrey, Mexico
Home schooled

Started a chiropractic marketing and management company at seventeen years of age

Currently runs chiropractic clinics and is a realtor in Minnesota and Wisconsin

2004 founded Wealth.com, an interactive real estate and investment resource based in Aliso Viejo, California, and Minneapolis, Minnesota

Kristi Frank
Raised in Lake Tahoe, Nevada
Worked as a blackjack dealer to pay for her college education
Degree in Industrial Engineering from the University of Southern California
Has broker's license and invests in real estate
Co-owner of Juliano's RAW, a restaurant in Santa Monica

Jason Curtis
Raised in Detroit, Michigan
B.A. in Advertising from Michigan State
President and founder of JMG Management, LLC
Owns rental units and properties

David Gould
Raised in Philadelphia
New York City venture capitalist in the healthcare sector
M.D. from Jefferson Medical College
M.B.A. from New York University

My hope is that you will use the book to apply each lesson to your work life and to support your aspirations of leadership. I hope also that the lessons will help you function better and find fulfillment. I focus on the personal—on knowing who you are and how power works in order to live and lead effectively.

CHAPTER ONE
"YOU'RE FIRED": VIEWS ON LEADERSHIP

Hiring an apprentice, Donald Trump wants a leader. Using the show as a guide, here are some observations on what makes a leader.

Accountability

In each task, Donald holds the project manager accountable for the performance of the team. When a task is completed, the teams must face Donald in the boardroom. Donald discusses the task with the teams and asks the project manager of the losing team to name the team members who most contributed to the loss. They then face Donald under tough scrutiny and one of them hears the now famous words, "You're Fired." Accountability is clearly assigned. The goal of each task is clear. Usually, money is the performance indicator. You win or you don't. There are no excuses, only results. If you lose, you are accountable and you go to the boardroom.

Smarts

In the first task, Donald said he would rather have a smart person making a great deal in a bad location, then an idiot making a bad deal in a great location. When he fired Troy, he said Troy just wasn't ready for a job with him. After the show, Donald offered to pay for Troy's college education. Smarts can come from education, experience, and the street. But, you must have them to succeed. As a task is given to the candidates, there is only a short time for them to deliver. The teams must be able to think on their feet, come up with a strategy, implement, and win. This takes smarts.

Not Crossing the Line

After successive wins by the women's team, Donald and Carolyn talked to them about using their sex appeal in every task. Donald told them they did not have to cross the line of sexuality to win. There are many ethical and other lines that can be crossed in business. Donald and Carolyn saw one being crossed and called the women on it.

Potential

In the very first boardroom meeting, Donald made his boardroom decision based on potential over performance. He told Troy that even though he was a lousy leader, he had potential. Troy was allowed to stay. Donald told Sam he would either do great or be a disaster. Donald hadn't figured out which way it would go yet. As Donald chose his apprentice, potential was factored in, but as the candidates narrowed, performance became the deciding factor. Donald also was considering the potential for candidates to fit into his organization. When he fired Amy, he said that she had done the best, but his people did not respect her. He thought this would make it hard to bring her into his organization.

Delivering

No question here. Donald wants the candidates to deliver. The whole set-up of the show reflects this. The dossier given at the start of each task clearly states what a team has to do to win. As Donald analyzes performance in the boardroom, he often makes delivering the bottom line. The team performs or it doesn't. The team that does not deliver sees one of its members fired. The team that wins sees its reward.

Skill

A candidate has to have skill. To be chosen to compete, candidates have to have proven their business skills. All the candidates are successful in their fields. In the lemonade-selling task, George and Donald talked about the skill of picking the right location. Kwame hadn't done it. Later in the season, Donald talked about Omarosa's lack of social skills. As Donald chose between Kwame and Bill, Donald said Bill had performed well and he was hired. Each task took skill to win.

Confidence

Donald expected the candidates to not only be confident, but to aggressively defend themselves and speak up. When Donald fired Kristi, he said he was disappointed that she didn't fight for herself. He fired Jessie for her passivity in the face of Omarosa's attacks. Omarosa was fired for having too many excuses. It takes confidence for a candidate to survive the boardroom. It takes confidence to perform tasks under intense scrutiny and pressure. You cannot be Donald's apprentice without having confidence.

CHAPTER TWO
LESSON ONE: TAKE RISKS

"Would I do it again? Absolutely!" —Heidi Bressler

With all it took for Heidi to compete on *The Apprentice,* she would do it again in a heartbeat. Heidi takes risks. You cannot succeed in business without taking them. What does this mean? It means that there will always be unknowns involved in business situations. You have to get comfortable with the possibility of loss. If you strive for absolute certainty or safety, you are doomed.

How do you get comfortable with risk? Start by assessing your own tolerance. What level of certainty or safety do you need to have? Here are several questions to consider.

In what areas can you tolerate no risk?
How comfortable are you with uncertainty?
What are you willing to risk in order to succeed?
What support structure do you need in order to risk?
What do you gain by increasing your tolerance for risk?
If you are afraid to risk, what is at the root of your fear?
How can you increase your tolerance for risk?

Risk is inherent in every aspect of *The Apprentice.* Starting with the competition to be selected for the show, candidates must convince producers and casting agents they are smart, aggressive, and better than the rest. In order to stand out, they have to distinguish themselves, sometimes looking very foolish. If they are chosen for the show, they must quit their jobs, for a 1:16 chance that they will succeed among a very talented group of candidates. Then, once the show begins, they must compete for Donald Trump and his staff in front of millions of viewers. As the field of candidates narrows, their skills are on trial and they are in the spotlight. I call this risk! You cannot become "The Apprentice" without embracing a series of risks. That's the bottom line.

What risks have you taken in your career and place of work? Many? A few? What has resulted from the risks you have taken? How have these experiences shaped your views regarding taking risks? Begin to define what your comfort zone is.

In the final competition of the first season of *The Apprentice*, we had a glimpse of Kwame's comfort zone as he dealt with Omarosa. Omarosa did not perform or keep Kwame adequately informed on the project. Kwame voiced his frustration with her, but said he could not fire her. Kwame explained that he was used to a work environment where people performed. Later, as Bill was chosen over Kwame as The Apprentice, Donald Trump asked Kwame why he didn't fire Omarosa. Kwame responded that he didn't know that was an option. Kwame did not step out of his comfort zone and it hurt him.

Once you know the boundaries of your comfort zone, begin to expand it. How can you do this? By taking risks. Start small, if you like. If you are uncomfortable with promoting yourself, step a bit outside of your comfort zone and tell someone of a success you have. If you are shy about promoting your ideas, speak up in meetings and to your superiors about what you think. As you do this, you will get more comfortable. Your comfort zone will begin to expand.

Then, begin to study risk. Observe people in your workplace. Try to define the elements of their comfort zone.

What level of risk are they comfortable with?
What seems to bring them out of their comfort zone?

Take it a step further and study leaders who have taken risks. (You could even start with Donald Trump, who has taken many risks and won and lost more than a few times!)

Note their qualities.
What motivated them to take the risks they did?
What price did they pay for taking the risks?
What rewards did they reap?
How did they prepare for taking risks?
Were they impetuous or calculating?
As you study risk-takers, which ones appeal most to you? Why?
How can you apply what you learn about them to your own life?
How can their stories help you develop a higher tolerance for risk?

Use their experiences to inform your own risk taking.

Now you have a foundation from which to begin taking risks in your career and workplace. Here are some tips to help you start.

Be Bold

Goethe put it this way: "Whatever you can do or dream, begin it. Boldness has genius, power, and magic in it." To be bold you are daring, somewhat fearless, you are conspicuous, you stand out, and you are assured and confident. It is the nature of success in the workplace that you must stand out. People have to see you. You must distinguish yourself. This is not always a comfortable thing for people. That's okay. You can acquire boldness.

Boldness creates wins on *The Apprentice*. In a task involving Trump Taj Mahal Hotel and Casino, the teams were asked to increase the casino's revenue by creating a game. Bill's team won that competition by being bold. Bill secured exclusive rights to escort V.I.P. gamblers from their special check-in line to his team's promotional area. Bill had nerve to think he could negotiate such a deal. It worked.

Let's look at some questions you can ask yourself about being bold. They are: Are you ready to be bold? What does it take? How do you find the courage to go beyond your comfort zone? How do you respond when you fall? And what are the rewards when you win?

Are You Ready to be Bold?

Boldness holds an allure for all of us. The limitations come when we set out to be bold. If you find yourself reticent to step into your boldness, here are a few things you can do: know where you are, be realistic but not restricting, and look at the rewards of being bold.

Know Where You Are

To know where you are, define your starting point. Take an inventory of your current situation. Look at your skills, your background, your location, your network, and your opportunities. This is what you start with. As you go on with your plans, you can use your starting point as a reference for where you are and what you need to pursue a goal. To experiment, pick a goal you have and measure it against your starting point. What is missing? What do you need to do to meet that goal?

> **What are the rewards of risk-taking?**
>
> higher stakes
> challenge
> growth
> winning

Be Realistic, but not Restricting

When it comes to boldness, this is a delicate balance. Restriction and boldness are opposites. But, you don't want your boldness to be foolhardy. Assess where you are against where you want to be. Allow your goals to be bold. The realism is in the planning. On *The Apprentice*, candidates have limited time to complete tasks. They want to be bold and they want to win. But their boldness must fit into the time period. What can they do with what they have? What are the boldest possible moves available to them?

Look at the Rewards of Being Bold

What better way to motivate than to see the rewards that are possible? When you are bold, you can realize your dreams. So, if you have a reticence about being bold, take some time to look at the rewards it can bring. Do some daydreaming. See your dream as realized. How has your life changed? What was available to you then that is not available now? Let these rewards become a motivator for your boldness.

Once you've tried these things, I hope you are ready to be bold. Jump in. Give it a shot.

What Does it Take?

Being bold takes commitment. First, you must focus. Identify what you need to do and stick to it. You must establish strong intent. You will do this no matter what. It is a priority. Boldness takes guts; muster the courage to do it. Humor helps so keep a sense of humor as you risk and learn.

Most of all, boldness requires movement. Take action. There is no substitute. And after you start, keep going. When you reach obstacles push through them. Get the support you need, but, stay in action. Don't stop the movement. Strong influences can deter you but if you stop, you may not resume again. See it through. Give up your excuses and act.

How Do You Find the Courage to Step Beyond Your Comfort Zone?

Courage is really about strength in the face of challenge, doubt, and stress. If you develop strength, you will find the courage to be bold. You must find the source of your strength. It could lie in commitment. Or, it could lie in faith. Or it could lie in endurance or tenacity. Think of times that you have been

> **How can I overcome fear?**
>
> commitment
> preparation
> knowledge
> nurturing

courageous. Where did you pull your strength from? Sometimes you need support to be strong. That's okay. Identify what support you need—a coach, a counselor, a friend, family. Be sure you have that support when you need it.

When I became a coach, I studied presentation skills with an excellent teacher, Jack Barnard. Jack is an actor and taught presentation from that point of view. He took someone like me with no acting skills and threw me into acting exercises. It was very effective. It got me out of my mind and back into the present moment. I could be fully present—mind, body, and spirit. Jack sometimes called himself, "an escort to the edge." The philosophy behind this was that if he could get people to the edge of their comfort zones, they could expand. By throwing me into the acting exercises, Jack was bringing me way out of my comfort zone. I am persistent. When he got me there I was going to stay. In the third of seven classes, I fell on my face. I froze in the middle of a presentation. But I would not give up. I came back to the fourth class and finished the course successfully. My persistence got me through and gave me courage. When I started the class, I was a bit nervous, but I knew I had to improve my skills. I convinced myself it would be safe. When I got to the edge of my comfort zone, I decided to go on.

Webster's Dictionary defines courage as "mental or moral strength to venture, persevere, and withstand danger, fear or difficulty." All these adversities could show up as you venture outside your comfort zone. Take some time to develop courage. The lion took the journey in *The Wizard of Oz*. You can too!

How Do You Respond When You Fall?

If you take risks, you will fall. It won't be all the time, but it will be some of the time. So first, accept now that you will experience some falls and failures. Here is a five-step plan to help you when you fall:

Step One: Pick Yourself Up

When you fall, pick yourself up and brush yourself off. Take care of any wounds you have. If your pride is hurt, soothe it. If you have caused any damage, repair it. Find your equilibrium to begin again. Give yourself the time you need to do this, but keep moving.

Step Two: Identify the Lessons

Once you are standing again, analyze what has happened. Enumerate the lessons that the fall or failure presents. You may have learned that there were flaws in your strategy. You may have learned something about another person. You may have learned how not to do something—that is valuable too! You may have learned that you do not have a skill that you need. Get back in movement by identifying your lessons learned.

Step Three: Give Yourself a Break

At this point, be good to yourself. Remind yourself that if you take risks, you will fail sometimes. Remind yourself that very successful people fail too. Find a way to nurture and be kind to yourself. Ease the negative effects of the fall. Give yourself a present. It may sound funny since you have fallen, but acknowledge yourself for having the courage to try. Acknowledge yourself for what worked. I'm sure that something did.

Step Four: Learn

This is the critical step. Take the first three steps and put them to use. Learn from what has happened. Take the lessons learned and apply them to your future. What will you do differently next time? What do you need to do to prepare for your next move? Do you need more skills? Do you need to rethink your strategy? Do you need to find new people to work with? Really ingrain these lessons in your head. Learning assures a positive result from your failure or fall.

Step Five: Start Again

Here it is again. Get in movement. It is the only way. Find a new project to focus on. Devise a new plan for the same project to succeed this time. Acquire a skill you need. Begin walking again.

What Are the Rewards When You Win?

When you take a risk and succeed you benefit. It feels good. You are happy. The project has brought you specific rewards. Revel in them. Beyond the project, you will experience other rewards. By winning, you have increased your confidence. You are smarter in knowing what it took to get the project done. You have increased your self-knowledge. You know more about how you work well. You have gained insights for the next time you risk. In every aspect, you are a winner.

Be Smart About it

If you want your risks to pay off, be smart. On *The Apprentice* it is a given that all the players are smart. Their smarts go beyond their innate intelligence, their schooling, and their experience to how they handle challenges. The tasks in the show are challenging. As soon as the teams receive them, they must get started. There isn't much time to read up on or change things. Teams have to take what they have, build a strategy, and get going.

In one task, Donald asked the teams to sell the work of an artist in an evening gallery showing. Donald warned the teams that the worth of art is subjective. It is not a cut and dried task. One team was split regarding which artist to promote. Some of the team had not seen the art. Nick, the project manager knew they had to get started. To some of his teammates chagrin, he made the decision himself. He was smart. They got going and Nick's team won. Nick knew he had to act or the team risked falling behind.

In contrast, the other team picked a complex and controversial artist. Some of the team members were not sure of their choice. They suffered for it. In light of the task—that the winner is the team that makes the most money, they made a poor decision and they lost. Donald said they lost because they did not believe in the product they were selling. Not too smart.

To be a player, you have to develop the smarts to back up your risk taking. Here are some factors in being smart: think, prepare, plan, re–think, and complete.

Think

When you decide to take a risk, make sure your brain is in gear. Be in the moment and at your best. When *The Apprentice* candidates get their assignment from Donald, they are on. They bring everything they have to succeeding. They have a lot at stake. Simply in the nature of risk, you have a lot at stake too. When you embark on a risk, engage your brain first.

Look at the whole picture before you.
What is the nature of your risk—what do you stand to win?
What do you stand to lose?
Who are the players?
What is needed to make the risk pay off?
What can stand in the way of your success?

Get smart about what is before you. Know all you can about your subject.

Yes, like the candidates on *The Apprentice*, you may have limited time. But, you still have to be smart. Find out what you can and make the best decisions possible. Put your full focus on what you need to do to maximize your chances of success.

Consider what can go wrong.
How will you handle it?
What do you need to make this work?

There are things you can do to improve how you think about risk. You can study risk. Learn more about the nature of risk. Study risk-takers. Understand what makes you uncomfortable about risk and work at recognizing and eliminating these things, so that you can think clearly. Then, practice. Think about risks you are considering taking. Identify several ways you can approach each risk. For example, if you are considering changing jobs. Create three scenarios for this change. One would be high risk, possibly quitting your current job immediately without a new one in place. The second would be medium risk, possibly changing fields. The third would be low risk, staying in your current job, until you have a new job in the same field.

To be smart about risk, make sure you think.

Prepare

It took me quite a few years to learn the value of preparation. I would frequently "wing it" in meetings or starting on projects. I would not do this carelessly though; I knew my field. I knew my strengths and weaknesses. I would read the necessary documentation before a meeting. Most times, it would work. Sometimes it wouldn't. But when it didn't, I seldom saw the cause in lack of preparation. I would attribute problems to a person's agenda or something that surprised me.

When I started my first business, I saw that a deeper level of preparation was possible. My business partner was very successful in her career and I saw that she took her preparation far more seriously than I did. She was expert in environmental regulations. If we were meeting with a client, she would study her regulations again, even though she was expert already, with that particular client's needs or situation in mind. She would think out who would be at the meeting and how each could affect the outcome. She would think in advance of things we could offer, ideas, strategies or the like, to meet the client's needs. Although she was already smart and knew her field well, I began to see that her preparation gave her the extra edge that made her so successful.

When you are taking a risk, it is even more important that you prepare. When you are moving out of your comfort zone, it is sometimes easier to misstep. I have a preparation tool that has worked well for my clients when they are taking a risk or going out of their comfort zone. If they are going to a meeting or beginning a task and have fear or concern about how they will do, we use this tool.

The first element is to identify who they are as they undertake the task. I ask them to list how they want the other parties involved to see them. This could be a statement of their credentials, or strengths. For example, they could say, I am a scientist with sixteen years experience, strong communication skills, and high creativity.

The second element is to identify two or three goals they have for the meeting or task. For example, to show the project group I have what it takes and to be asked to join the project as a manager. The purpose of this preparatory task is really to ground the client in who they are, and what they want to accomplish. Often, clients write down the two elements and read them just before the meeting. It focuses them and builds their confidence.

Never underestimate the advantage preparation gives you in undertaking a risk.

> *"I've been working for this my whole life."*
> —Bill Rancic, the first Apprentice

Plan

Planning allows you to organize your actions to your advantage. It aids you in thinking out what is before you. When the candidates on *The Apprentice* receive a task from Donald, the first thing they do is plan. They must. They have to organize their team to work effectively towards the goal. They have to set the steps that will get them where they want to go.

As you undertake a risk, develop a plan. Your plan will aid you in thinking out the nuts and bolts of what you must do, who must be involved, and how you will do it. A plan also helps you develop your strategy for winning. As you determine the nuts and bolts of your plan, you will see your strategy emerge and you can evaluate if it will work or if it needs to be fine-tuned. As you develop your plan, you may choose to use one of the many planning tools available. Two examples are software tools with flow charts to help you lay out your ideas and SWOT analysis where you lay out the strengths, weaknesses, opportunities, and threats involved.

In the plan, clearly define your goals. What do you want to accomplish? Be specific regarding your goal and how you will get there. Work out the timing, by developing a timeline for the undertaking from start to finish. Develop measures for success. There is a popular saying that you manage what you measure. What will be your indicators of success? Measures are developed for every step of the plan. They will allow you to determine if you are on track toward success. With measures you have your plan set—you are ready to begin!

Planning can often be overlooked, but not without peril. Sometimes people are so anxious to get started, they do not want to take the time to plan. Some feel you only learn through action. But, planning helps you avoid missteps that could slow you down. There is nothing that says you cannot plan fast and thoroughly. Make the effort to plan and you actually will be streamlining your project. Can you imagine Donald Trump building a skyscraper without a plan?

Re-Think

Now you have started your project; it is underway. As you progress, look back at your plan on at least a weekly basis. Chart your progress on your measures with everyone involved in the project. If you are doing a project on your own, check them yourself. Get trusted colleagues to give you their thoughts on places where you are stuck or not meeting your measures.

It is important to re-think your plan and strategy as you move along. Conditions inevitably change. Surprises arise. Blind adherence to a plan does not serve you. Your plan must be a living, flexible document. You must be adaptable.

Donald Trump may have the best idea for a residential development. Assume he has an excellent plan, outlining every step along the way. One thing he has planned for is approval by the New York City Planning Commission. He knows how the process works and has planned for each step involved. However, community opposition arises to the project in an area that Donald's team did not anticipate. Here is a place where the team will re-think the plan, so that they can move forward towards success. Re-thinking and reorienting allows you to reach your goals whatever happens. You may end up revising your goals, but you have to plan within the context of the real world.

Sometimes, the blows to your project can seem fatal. At that point, you may see the writing on the wall. Okay, that's life, but you see it and now can decide how to proceed. When Donald gave the candidates a task of managing one shift of a pedicab company, we saw this in action. The team that brought in the most money for an eight-hour shift would win. The Protégé team came up with incentive and pre-paid card programs. Versacorp decided to sell advertising on the back of the pedicabs. At one point in the day, the Protégé team saw one of Versacorp's pedicabs with advertising on the back. They were stunned. Troy said, "We were looking up the ass of a dead dog with fleas!" In the end Versacorp beat Protégé almost ten times over.

Let's hope you do not encounter many fatal blows like this one. But when you do make the best of it. More often, you will encounter situations that require fine-tuning. If your team and you are looking regularly at your plan and charting your progress against your measures, you will have time to adjust your plan and proceed.

As you risk, don't forget the importance of your plan. It is your navigator through calm and stormy weather, and charts your course to success.

Complete

This seems obvious, yes? But, it amazes me how often it is overlooked or given short shrift. On *The Apprentice,* completion is built in. At the end of each task, the two teams go to the boardroom and meet Donald and his team. The progress of each team is given. The winner is identified. Then, the losing team must have a separate meeting with Donald in the boardroom, as the winning team enjoys their prize. In this meeting, Donald and his team review the project and why the team lost. They ask for the team members' views and demand accountability.

You clearly mark the beginning of a project. Now mark the end. It is not just for the sake of doing it. Completion is about fulfillment and bringing to a final state. You do not want to leave loose ends. You want to learn all you can. You want to be done and to move freely to your next project. If you do not complete, any number of things can happen. You can find something boomerang back to you long after the project is over. You can forget an obligation you did not fulfill in the project or something left undone. You can leave the project without its lessons learned.

Build completion into your plan. Whether you succeed or fail, you must complete. You can even add a debrief. Look at what happened.

> What lessons do you learn from it?
> What did you do well?
> What did you do poorly?
> What did/didn't you anticipate?
> How will you do things differently in the future?

At the end of your project, tie it up in a very nice bow of analysis, all tasks complete, all good things rewarded, and all that needs it corrected. Then you walk away free.

Completion is your closing. Make it as important as every other step in your plan.

Aim High

Andre Godin said, "The quality of our expectations determines the quality of our actions." What are the expectations of the candidates for *The Apprentice*? From the beginning of the casting calls, every single candidate is aiming high. In my research for this book, I came across a web site prepared by Marty Kotis, an applicant for the second season of *The Apprentice*. The site address was www.realapprentice.com. On the site, Marty made a pitch to be chosen as a candidate. He even had a link to an e-mail, which visitors could send to support his bid! I call that aiming high.

If you are going to take risks, why not go for the best? Aiming high is a trait of true leaders. Donald Trump's father made millions developing real estate in the outlying boroughs of New York City. Donald aimed even higher-he set his sights on Manhattan, the heart of the city. Yes, aiming high increases the positives and negatives of the risks. But, aiming high is not an invitation to be foolhardy. It is an invitation to believe that you can go for the best.

Here are some questions to consider as you set your sights high.

Can you find a good reason not to aim high?
What holds you back from aiming high?
What do you gain by aiming high?
What do you lose by not aiming high?

Give some thought to these questions. Your answers can set you on the path to aiming high. If your answers are negative, do what you need to convert them to positive.

By aiming high, you are believing in yourself. You are telling the world that you matter. Not only will it make a difference in your life, but I bet it will inspire those around you to do the same. Here are some things to consider as you plan to aim high: want the very best, no limits, walk the path step-by-step, and realize that life goes up and down

> *"I like thinking big. I always have. To me it's very simple: if you're going to be thinking anyway, you might as well think big."*
> —Donald Trump, *The Art of the Deal*

Want the Very Best

What are your dreams and aspirations? What do you really want in life? That's the start. Have you allowed yourself to dream? Begin now. Take some time just to dream. Picture the life that will bring you happiness and fulfillment. When Donald Trump describes the style of his buildings, he speaks of his own tastes for bronze and marble and how he loves expansive views. He has built his wants, as well as those of his customers, into his designs. It works. Donald's buildings are hot commodities in New York City.

In my work, I have learned that I need to spend time daydreaming. The process of visualizing and imagining a good life helps you get in touch with what you want. It gives you a sense of how you will feel when you have it. It helps you define what is best for you. Try doing some daydreaming. Dream of the things in life: your family life, your career, your friendships, your fun and recreation, and even your philanthropy.

What do you gain by thinking small? Do you have an answer to this question that satisfies you? When you think small, what feeling is this based on? My guess is you will find a diminishment or lack of confidence at the bottom of it. Believing you deserve the very best is not easy for everyone. But, you do deserve the best and the only way to get it is to go for it. Let go of any thinking that does not support your getting the best.

Want the best for others too. That is also a trait of true leaders. Wanting the best for others will make your scope bigger. People will want to follow your leadership. They will see your genuine desire for their betterment. They will support you and work harder for you.

Wanting the very best sets your sights high. It makes all things possible. It stretches you to your highest good. It uses all you have to give. It creates a feeling of contagious optimism. It radiates out to those around you.

So, as you consider aiming high, go for the very best. If you are going to risk at all, why not do it best?

No Limits

As you aim high, I suggest you allow no limits as you begin. Sure, limits will show up along the way. But, if you set limitations in your foundation, it will be very hard to let them go.

I am sure every candidate on *The Apprentice* is going for the top spot. They put their all into being chosen. Can you imagine a candidate saying I will go for number two? I don't think so. There is a limitation. In reality they know that only one is chosen. But this limitation, if accepted, would defeat them. They believe they can do it. They set out with no limits.

What do you need to start out with no limits? Here are some ideas.

Confidence. Believe that you can do it. Believe that your skills, opportunity, help from others, and good fortune will all come together in your favor.

Open Eyes. Begin with your eyes open. Accept the reality of the situation. For example, if you are going for a spot on *The Apprentice* see that there are hundreds of thousands there with you as you start.

Hope. Hope plays here. *Webster's* defines hope as "desire accompanied by expectation or belief in fulfillment."

A Sense of Possibility. This is a feeling that, no matter the outcome, you are on an adventure. All things are possible and great things may come.

Commitment. This is essential. Nothing is achieved—particularly great things—without commitment.

So, as you set out, allow no limits. Have a good time with it. Picture yourself achieving your goal and the wonderful things that come with it!

Walk the Path Step–by-Step

You have to start somewhere. It is in action that dreams are realized. What is your first step? Identify it and take it. There is tremendous power in your first step.

As your project progresses, take it step-by-step. You cannot avoid this. You may skip a few steps along the way, but most of the steps must be taken to get where you want to go. In the very first task of *The Apprentice*, Donald asked the candidates to sell lemonade. No one was going to win, unless they came together with their team. They were dependent on each other. Once their teams were together they had steps to take to find a location, gather materials, get out there to sell, actually sell, and have a strategy to win. Each step had to be taken and right away. They only had one chance.

In your planning, identify all necessary steps, what you need for each, and who will take them. Look at each step as a building block.

Complete each step well. Identify any additional steps that become necessary and take them. Eliminate any frivolous steps that do not lead to success. Do not allow yourself to detour, stay on the path.

Taking a project step-by-step is not glamorous; it can get a bit boring. But resign to it. Make it as fun an endeavor as you can. Be up about it and look to each step as a challenge. Keep your sights on the end point—step-by-step you will get there.

> *"I try never to leave myself too exposed."*
> —Donald Trump, *The Art of the Deal*

Realize That Life Goes Up and Down

With all this said about aiming high and wanting the best, there is another equal truth. Life goes up and down. It just isn't so that you are always on top. Part of aiming high is knowing that there will be lows. It is a natural movement. Minimize the impact of the lows by realizing they will be there. Do not let the lows define you. Master them and rise.

How will you handle the ups and downs as you reach for the top? I suggest a few things. First, accept that they exist and that you will experience them. Second, see the positives in the lows when they come. What can it teach you? What must you improve to reach the top? How have they increased your knowledge and sharpened your skills? Third, start moving up. Identify what you need to do to get going again. Acknowledge the realities of each low, but get in motion again. Set your view again towards the top. You will get there.

Accept Uncertainty

On *The Apprentice,* each candidate sets out within a myriad of unknowns.

Will they be selected for the show?
What is Donald really looking for?
How will they interact with Donald's staff?
Who will their team members be?
Can they handle the spotlight and the competition?

What will it be like to live together?
What tasks will they be given?
Who will get fired?
Who will win?

If candidates get lost in trying to figure out these uncertainties, they will take precious focus and energy away from performing well on the show. They have to move on and deal with what is before them.

Like it or not, life involves uncertainty. As a society we do our best to avoid it, but it is still there. It is an illusion to think you can control every aspect of your life. In the unknown there can be insecurity or fear. But, the unknown also brings adventure and possibility. It is to your benefit to accept uncertainty.

Why does accepting uncertainty matter? By acknowledging that uncertainty exists, you are accepting a truth. If you try to deny its existence, you will spend much effort building a fortress of security that will not work. If you fear the unknown, it begins to control you. You build your life around denying its existence. You seek security and try to avoid change.

Allowing that uncertainty exists is living life within its true meaning. You treasure what you have. You accept that you do not know your future. You do your best to create stability, but you allow for change and the unexpected in your life—you do your best to prepare for it. It may not be an ideal existence, but you are living in the truth of what is.

In accepting uncertainty, you see life as it is and can make your judgments accordingly. As you take a risk, you can acknowledge the presence of uncertainty and do your best to deal with it. You can build strategies to minimize the negative effects of uncertainty. You can build assumptions to make the best decision possible.

To lead well and gain the confidence of those around you, you must know how to handle uncertainty. Now we will discuss some things you can do. They are: get comfortable with the unknown, set your assumptions, find support, and accept its presence.

"The unknown is what is. And to be frightened of it is what sends everybody scurrying around chasing dreams, illusions, war, peace, love, hate, all that. Unknown is what is. Accept that it's unknown and it's plain sailing."
—John Lennon

Get Comfortable With the Unknown

Find a way to enjoy the ride. If the unknown won't go away, you might as well find a way to deal with it. The unknown can be exciting. In the face of the unknown anything is possible. Ask yourself what can happen now, what might the unknown bring, and what possibilities are now open to me. As a risk-taker, think of the advantages you will have if you are comfortable with the unknown. Think of the stress and anxiety you will be saving yourself from.

Start getting comfortable by examining the presence of the unknown in your life today. Are there unknowns in your work life? What are they? Some examples may be that your company is downsizing and everyone's future is uncertain, uncertainties may exist in the economy or your market sector that could affect your business, or a parent or child is ill and you may have to devote a serious amount of time to their care. These examples can create stress and anxiety, understandably. In examining unknowns, there can also be exciting situations such as you've just been offered a fabulous new job that you will have to prove yourself in, you are beginning to find your passion and are not sure where to go with it, or there's a possibility of getting a contract for your business that dwarfs what you have gotten so far. Knowing what unknowns exist helps your comfort level with them.

Adopt a philosophy about the unknown that works for you. You may decide on a philosophy that you will accept the unknown, but will do your best to deal effectively within it. Or, you may develop a philosophy that says you will not let fear of the unknown get the better of you. Find your comfort level with the unknown and get on with life.

One thing that may help your comfort level is to acknowledge what the unknown teaches you. You can use its lessons in decision-making and risk-taking. Bottom line: make the best of it.

Set Your Assumptions

In the face of uncertainty, prepare the best you can. If you are sailing around the world, weather presents great uncertainties. So, you make sure you have extra sails, good navigational instruments, and excellent communication systems. As you face uncertainty, you can improve your situation by developing the assumptions upon which you will proceed. Assumptions are statements that at the present time, appear to be true. In our sailing example, your assumption is that a storm may arise, so you prepare for it.

When I worked at the U.S. Environmental Protection Agency, my division was responsible for decisions regarding whether to take certain pesticides off the market. Our decisions could have significant environmental and economic impacts. We frequently had to make decisions based on conflicting scientific studies. Two studies looking at the same pesticide would have differing conclusions regarding its health effects. As we prepared our decision documents, a great deal of time was spent in developing our assumptions. These assumptions would lead to our decision. If our decision was challenged, much of the ensuing discussion focused on the assumptions the agency made. I ran a policy unit in the division. One of our major projects was to write a policy paper on how we could make effective decisions in the midst of uncertainty. Our assumptions became the backbone of our decisions when irrefutable facts were not available.

Once you have developed your assumptions, proceed based on them. Adjust accordingly if an assumption is proven false. Develop skill in identifying your assumptions and you will have an effective ally to help you deal with uncertainty.

Find Support

With all my promoting of accepting uncertainty, I do recognize that it is not easy. So, as you proceed get some support. Delving into the unknown is a hero's journey. You deserve allies and guidance along the way. Here are several things you can do.

Read

Find books about dealing with the unknown. Books about dealing with your fears are appropriate too. Reading will give you guidance along the way.

Friends

Find friends who will support you as you take risks and confront the unknown. This can be personal friends, colleagues, coaches, or professional mentors. Have someone to talk to about how you feel. Accept the guidance of those who have walked the path before you. Value their insights regarding what you are facing.

Spiritual Teachings

There is a spiritual aspect of facing the unknown. Through a religion, a spiritual community, or a spiritual teacher, form your foundation of faith to face the unknown. Or perhaps, support is gained in your faith in yourself. Build that faith.

Nurture

In times of stress or moving out of your comfort zone, increase your self-nurturing. This is essential. Fear or discomfort with the unknown can wear you down. However you nurture yourself, do it more.

Accept its Presence

How do you truly accept that uncertainty exists in your life? It is not an easy task. Here are some ways to begin.

> Allow that there are things you do not know.
> Accept that these things can affect your life and the lives of those who are dear to you.
> Identify what you can do to ease any fear you have around uncertainty.

Resolve to face uncertainty in your life in the best possible way.

By acknowledging that uncertainty exists, you free yourself from fear. At times, you may still be afraid. But, you will be living life in its truth. There is no better choice.

RECAP
Be bold. Allow yourself to step out of your comfort zone.
Be smart about it. Think everything out, prepare, and then jump.
Aim High. Want the very best. Do not let anything limit you.
Accept Uncertainty. Get comfortable with the unknown.

EXERCISES
1. Select a task that is given on *The Apprentice*. Identify the inherent risks in the task. Create three ways to approach the task—high, medium, and low risk. For each approach, identify what you need to make it a win.

2. Pick a candidate on *The Apprentice*. Create an imaginary scenario of how that person found the courage to apply to be on the show.

3. Prepare for a hot air balloon trip around the world. Analyze the risks involved, and how you will handle them.

CHAPTER THREE
LESSON TWO: BE YOURSELF

"I made it, Mama!" —Troy McClain

After the conclusion of the first season of *The Apprentice*, several of the candidates appeared on CNN's *Larry King Live*. Donald Trump phoned in to speak with them. When he spoke to Troy, Donald said he heard that Troy wanted to go to college, and Troy agreed that he did. When Donald offered to pay his way through school, Troy was stunned. He said he wanted to go to Harvard and then get his MBA from Wharton. As it sunk in, Troy looked at the camera and said, "I made it, Mama!"

Troy was an audience favorite. Many people coming onto *The Apprentice*, as a candidate, would have adopted a persona of success that mirrored Donald Trump's—sophistication, confidence, and city smarts. Troy came onto the show 100 percent himself. Without a college education or big city style, he made it into the late stages of the competition. He speaks with a twang, wears a funny hat, but is smart as a whip. He knows who he is and what he can do. He knows how to use who he is to his best advantage. He is open regarding his idolization of Donald Trump through the years. To some, he may seem hokey, but Troy is the real thing.

Are you being yourself in your work? If your answer is yes—great! If your answer is no—why not? Sometimes, people think it is a disadvantage to be yourself in the work world. I disagree. If you are not yourself, then who are you? Are you imitating someone else? Are you living according to someone else's standards? If you are, you are building a false foundation. The best route to true leadership is to start from who you are. From there, you can highlight your strengths and improve on your weaknesses. By doing this, you develop a true style of leadership—one that is uniquely yours.

Candidates for *The Apprentice* are highly successful professionals. They are a diverse group. It is fair to say they each have developed their personal leadership style. Certainly, Donald Trump has used his strengths to develop a very strong brand for his enterprises. As the candidates come together for a particular task, they bring their own, unique perspectives to create a strong team. Sometimes their views and styles clash, but that's not our focus in this chapter. What we are looking at is that being yourself is the best place to start as you develop as a leader.

In your place of work, how do you approach this task of being yourself? First, take an inventory of your strengths and weaknesses and analyze them.

> What strengths do you bring to your work?
> What weaknesses have hindered you in your work?
> As you identify them, take a look at their foundations.
> For a strength: how was it developed?
>> Is it innate in who you are or did you have to work at it?
>> Regarding that strength, how can you highlight or enhance it to your advantage?
>
> For a weakness: where does it come from?
>> Is it rooted in an insecurity or lack of confidence?
>> Is it something you can change? If you can't change it, (say you want to rise up the ranks of management, but the CEO only promotes people who went to the United States Naval Academy and you did not) is it time to find another work environment?

Second, take a look at who you are at work today.
   Are you being yourself?
   If not, why not?
   What factors make you stray from who you are?
   If you are being yourself, is it working to your advantage?

You have to decide if who you are fits with your profession and place of work. Why swim upstream? If your work requires you to be someone you are not, why are you there? Once you take a look, identify anything that you want to change. Are there aspects of yourself that will help you get ahead? Are there aspects of yourself that deflect from your leadership?

In a task on the show where teams had to renovate and rent an apartment, Troy used one of his strengths, as a shrewd negotiator, to his advantage. Each team would see the same two apartments. They would then negotiate which apartment each would work with. Troy and Katrina negotiated for their respective teams. Troy wouldn't divulge which apartment he wanted. He overheard Katrina saying to her team that the second had more potential. Then Katrina suggested they both write down on a piece of paper which apartment they wanted. Troy refused and said he wanted what Katrina wanted. Katrina was furious, realizing Troy had overheard her speaking to her team, and said Troy was unethical. They ended up flipping a coin—not the best form of negotiating. Troy had succeeded in getting Katrina off balance. She was still protesting as she went into the boardroom, as part of the losing team, to meet Donald. Katrina accused Troy of being unethical. Donald's view was that Katrina had just been duped.

Once you know your strengths and weaknesses well, you have a place to start being yourself. Here are some tips to using who you are to your best advantage.

Authenticity

The word authentic means genuine, conforming to fact or reality, trustworthy, and corresponding with the truth. If you take that as a standard for yourself, it is a lofty one. But, if you put yourself on a path to authenticity, you are streamlining your path to leadership. Authenticity, being true to who you are, is an essential ingredient in leadership.

Let's look at authenticity on *The Apprentice*. Each candidate can only testify to his or her authenticity. But, we can take a look at them and offer our opinions. Who on the show do you believe is authentic? Who is not? Is Kwame authentic? He is highly educated, ambitious, and he has his own style. He knows himself and will acknowledge who he is if questioned. Is Omarosa authentic? Only she knows. I would ask her the following: Did you want to work hard? Why were you playing basketball after you were hurt and said you could not work? Did you want to be a lightning rod in the group—is that who you are? Is Sam authentic? He wore his high ambition on his sleeve. He wanted to win. He had his own unique style and was not embarrassed by what he did. Is Heidi authentic? Heidi's personality said this is who I am, take it or leave it.

Now, let's discuss some aspects of authenticity. They are: conditionings and experiences, knowing your values, living true to who you are, and accepting yourself.

Conditionings and Experiences

In my work with clients, some of them encounter an arduous road to their authenticity. They may have years of family or social conditioning

---

What makes them authentic leaders?

Ronald Reagan
A great communicator
Knew what he stood for
Passionate in beliefs

Joe Gibson
Inspires the team
Goes the distance with team
Asks for 100 percent

Oprah Winfrey
Empathic
Knows herself
Visionary

that told them to be a certain way. These conditionings have masked who they really are. Others have to confront a lack of self-esteem. They do not think they are good enough; they see negatives in who they are. Others may have been beaten down by their work experiences. They encountered a boss who said they weren't good enough. They experienced failures. The road to authenticity involves removing the barriers created by conditionings or experiences.

How does one go about removing these conditionings or experiences? First, acknowledge that they exist. Know what they are and how they came about. Think about your childhood. Look at your conditionings.

> What did your parents and others in your life tell you about what you must be?
> Were you told to conform?
> Were you told to pursue a "secure" career and not take risks?
> Were you told you could be anything you put your mind to be?
> Were you told that your creativity would never earn you money?
> How did you feel when you heard these things?
> Did you accept them as truths?
> Did you feel conflicted because you wanted to go another way?
> Examine this and identify, specifically, the conditionings that influenced who you are today.

> Now look at your life experiences.
> As a child, were you encouraged to be yourself?
> Were you given challenges?
> Were you acknowledged for your strengths and achievements?
> How did school go for you?
> Did you feel smart or did you feel "less than"? Why?
> What happened when you began work?
> What kind of job did you have?
> Were you mentored or did you go it on your own?
> How did you do?

How has your career been?
Have you succeeded or do you perceive yourself a failure?
Examine this and identify, specifically, the experiences that influenced who you are today.

You must know how conditionings and experiences influence who you are today. Acknowledging them and letting go of what no longer serves you is a powerful step in establishing your authenticity.

> *"Be honest with yourself and do what you are comfortable doing instead of concerning yourself with what you think others want you to do."*
> —Robert J. Birnbach, President/CEO of Primordium Holdings, LLC quoted in *The Way to the Top,* Donald Trump

Knowing Your Values

Another aspect of authenticity is truth. It is a lofty question, but what is your truth? What does it mean to be who you are? One way to begin to answer this question is to identify your values. By values, I mean the essence of who you are, the essential nature of you. When I trained at the Coaches Training Institute (CTI), they put strong emphasis on values being a foundation of coaching. Our clients needed to know their values and act according to them.

You can begin by asking yourself some questions, based on my work at CTI. Here they are:

Think of a time in your life when you were very happy.
What was happening then?
What made you happy?
What values were being honored?
Think of a time when you were angry.
What happened?
What caused the anger?
What values were not being honored?

Sometimes, life can be okay without a certain value being honored, but when you do honor that value, life is magical. Can you think of a value you have where this applies?

Create a scenario where a value you have cannot be honored.

What must you have in life besides food, clothing, and shelter?

Once you've answered these questions, glean your values from them. What do you see in your answers that tell you what your values are? An example could be if someone in identifying a time they were angry, described a situation where a boss prevented them from telling the truth about a situation, their value may be honesty or integrity.

Now let's go two more places with this. First, look at your list of values. Prioritize the top ten. Yes, it's hard, but you will face situations where you have to choose what's really important to you and setting priorities help you do this. Second, rate the level at which you are honoring each value in your present life. Do this on a scale of one to ten—one meaning not honoring the value at all—ten meaning fully honoring the value. For example, if freedom is a value and you are working as a sole proprietor of a home-based business, you could be honoring that value at an eight or nine.

Have fun identifying your values. Honor them in your life. My guess is that your values create a beautiful picture of who you are!

Living True to Who You Are

When you have identified how your conditionings and experiences have influenced you and identified your values, it is time to live who you are. What do I mean by that? I mean being true to your values and living life authentically.

To begin, think about what an authentic life is for you. No boundaries—let your imagination go. What would your life look like? What would you be doing? What people would be in your life? What would your work be? What emotions would you be feeling? What would you do in your leisure time?

Then, take a look at your present day life. Identify what parts of your life are authentic. Why do you consider them authentic? Look at what parts of your life are not true to your authentic self. Why have you deemed them so? This analysis will give you a roadmap to creating authenticity in your life.

Now develop a plan to get to your authentic life. Of the elements you deemed authentic, what can you do to enhance them? Create a timeline to get it done. For the elements you deemed not authentic, ask yourself the following questions.

> Why is this element in your life?
> Is it a result of a conditioning or experience?
> If the element, such as a job, were to go away, what would the consequences be?
> Will it be easy or difficult to let go of this element? Why?
> What do you gain and lose by letting go of it?

Proceed now to prepare a plan to let these non-authentic elements go. Be practical. It may take some time for some. Create a timeline as part of your plan. Get support for doing this. Set a strong intent and fly to your authenticity!

Accepting Yourself

Now you have a true picture of living an authentic life. You know how your conditionings and experiences have affected you. You have identified your values. You know what it is to live true to who you are. The next step is to fully accept yourself. You are not a perfect being. The good comes along with the bad. You may falter. Things in the past may not have gone the way you wanted them to. It may take time to create authenticity.

Give yourself some credit—you are on your way. You will get there. Don't beat yourself up. What does it mean to accept yourself? It may mean giving up perfectionism. Or, you can like the picture of your life with both its good and its bad. You can highlight and acknowledge what you already have accomplished. Say, "I'm okay." Believe that you will get where you want to go.

Accepting yourself is key to reaching the top of this mountain to authenticity. If you demean or doubt yourself, you are using valuable energy for an unworthy purpose. If you focus on what has passed or what is impossible to change, you set a foolhardy task. Accept exactly where you are and start from there. Convince yourself that now is what you have and it's a good starting point. You can get anywhere you want to go. Accept who you are as you proceed on this journey.

In an interview with Michael Toms of New Dimensions Radio, the mythologist, Joseph Campbell, told a story from the philosopher Nietzsche. The story says we begin life as a camel taking the burdens of society on our backs. At a certain point, the camel goes out, alone, into the desert. When the camel reaches the desert, it transforms into a lion. The ferocity of the lion is equivalent to the burden on the camel's back. The lion is then given a task to slay the dragon named "Thou Shalt." The dragon has two thousand scales. On each scale is a conditioning or rule of society. The lion must slay the dragon one scale at a time. When the lion has slain the dragon it transforms into a child and begins to live life for the first time.

Authenticity is a key ingredient of true leadership. Be true to who you are. Use your traits to their full advantage. Say goodbye to the parts of you that are not true to your essential nature.

Living Out Loud

One of my favorite quotes is from the artist, Emile Zola. It is, "I am here to live out loud." Living out loud is about loving who you are and bringing yourself out to the world. It is not about shrinking, or lack of confidence, or feeling inadequate. It is about standing tall and being proud to say, "This is who I am."

I think it is a fair statement to say that Donald Trump lives out loud. He is known around the world. He flashes his name on buildings, planes, and merchandise. He lives well and lets the world see. I would also say that *The Apprentice* candidates are well on their way to living out loud. They have the guts to compete against thousands. They want to show Donald who they are. They want to stand out in the world. What about Amy? Do you think she lives out loud? I would say so. What about Omarosa? Yes, that's a given.

No judgment comes with living out loud. It is a state of being. It is not about specifics. It is a quality. It is the ability and desire to be seen in the world. It is about letting the world know you are here.

There are numerous ways to live out loud. Find the ones that are right for you. Here are some things to consider. Do you want to live out loud? What fits? How will you do it? What are the risks and benefits?

Do You Want to Live Out Loud?

There are different strokes for different folks. How do you want to live your life? As a leader, people do need to see you, but there are varying degrees of this. There are high profile leaders and low-key leaders. You can begin to answer this question by taking a look at leaders of the past and present in this world. To what degree did they each live out loud?

Jack Welch is a highly successful leader. He is revered for his management of General Electric Company. He lives out loud. He has written books on management, he speaks around the world, and he is seen in the right places. He has decided to live out loud.

Dick Cheney lives a bit less out loud. As vice president in the Bush Administration and in roles in prior administrations, he wields a tremendous amount of power. But he stays decidedly low profile. He isn't looking for the spotlight.

Mother Theresa was a humble nun who chose to live out loud. It is possible that living out loud was not essential to her nature. But, she chose to raise her own profile in order to raise the profile of the plight of the poor and the need to help them.

How do you want to lead? What do you want to accomplish? For what you want to do, what level of living out loud is right? Can you do it? Think of something you want to do. Then try an experiment. Imagine doing it at different levels of living out loud. One level may be working quietly behind the scenes, only seen by the key decision makers. Another level may be raising your profile to bring attention to yourself or your cause. Analyze each level as to your personal level of comfort in it, and its effectiveness in accomplishing what you want. This will help you determine how you want to live out loud.

What Fits?

It is important that your style fit who you are. On *The Apprentice,* if Bill patterned himself totally after Donald Trump, it wouldn't fit. He has many of Donald's attributes—smarts, style, and ability. But his style is mellower—more low key. If Sam decided to stay in the background and work behind the scenes, he may not be noticed. Sam put himself out there in a big way and we all saw him.

As you decide on your level of living out loud, stay keenly aware of how your wants, style, and abilities fit that level. Ask yourself a few questions

- Do you like the spotlight?
- Can you handle a lot of attention on your strong and weak points, your successes and your failures?
- Do you need recognition?
- Do you prefer working behind the scenes?
- What gets things done best—are you a tortoise or a hare? How will that play in the spotlight?
- What comes along with the spotlight? Can you handle it?
- Will you change your level of living out loud for different situations? Can you? Will the world let you once you're out there?

You have choice here. What level of living out loud is right for you? Study leaders. Study what comes along with living out loud. You can experiment with it in small ways. Pick a project and create approaches to it at three different levels of living out loud. Which is most effective for you? Living out loud doesn't work unless it fits.

How Will You Do it?

You want to live out loud? Then just do it. Begin now. Choose ways to experiment with living out loud. You can start big or small. If you have your own business, you could join a networking group where you are asked to give a thirty-second pitch for your business at each meeting. Prepare your pitch, practice and give it. You are living out loud. In your workplace you could say something you've wanted to say for awhile but have lacked the courage. Or, you could show your coworkers a skill you have as you work together on a project. What are some ways you can live out loud? Living out loud is about not holding back—about showing yourself to the world. You can be outrageous or you can be subtle. Do what's right for you.

When you try living out loud, take time to examine what you did.

How did it feel to live out loud?
What did you have to do to make it work for you?
Did you do all you had to?
How did it go?
Did you have a result in mind?
Did you accomplish it?
How did people react?
How did you respond to their reactions?
What did you learn about living out loud?

By living out loud you are allowing yourself to be seen. Is that comfortable for you? Sometimes people want to take the safe road. Keep your head down and you'll stay out of trouble. That may be true, but leaders are seen, there's no getting around that. If it is uncomfortable for you to be seen, search for the source of that feeling. Once you identify the source, work on it. Perhaps it goes against your early conditioning. Perhaps you have experienced being seen and negative things have occurred. Perhaps you are shy by nature. Whatever the source is, acknowledge it and begin to change that feeling and replace it with a desire to be seen. Do not force it. It is an exploration. Sometimes change takes time.

Living out loud has its own rewards. But to do it you must be seen. Begin now to be seen. Let the world know who you are.

The Risks and Benefits

As I developed my own leadership abilities, I began to look at what happens to people who put their head above the crowd. I collected articles that illustrate this. This examination taught me about a very important aspect of leadership. There are risks and benefits to living out loud and leading.

Think of some of the high profile people in the world today. You know both good and bad about them, yes? What happens as someone begins to rise as a leader? Here are some of the things I found in my examination. As a leader rises, people are drawn to them. There is a magnetic sense in their being. They may have written a book, been involved in a major news event, created something, or made their voice heard in a big way. People listen to them; they want more. They like the attention and the opportunity to have influence in the world. Some respond to this by developing a large ego. Others handle it humbly or with aplomb. At some point in the leader's career, negativity comes into the picture. Today, it seems almost inevitable that the leader will deal with criticism, a scandal, an invasion of their privacy, or something similar. Part of this is that there is a natural ebb and flow to life. Another aspect of this is that our society tends to shoot down our heroes. Why is this? I'm not sure, but I've seen it in action many times.

With the risks of leading and living out loud, benefits come too. Living out loud gives you a place in the world. Your voice is heard when you want it to be. It allows the world to know you. You have the opportunity to make the world a better place or to influence it in some way. You can accomplish what you set out to do. You can learn more about life on a bigger stage. You can make a difference in the world. You will not live a life that is unexpressed. You will know you gave it your all. You will not be plagued by "what if" or fall into a bitter view of the world because of what you were not able to do.

Have fun reaching a point where you can live out loud. I bet the world is waiting for you and what you have to give.

Have Confidence

Confidence is an essential element of leadership. It is not ego, bravado, or in-your-face ways. Confidence is self-possession, knowing who you are, and presenting yourself with skill. Does Donald Trump have confidence? I think so—and not only by the way he carries himself. Donald Trump has shown self-confidence by what he believes he can do. He lets you know that he can build the tallest building, make the super-rich happy, and take on the giants in the casino world. He also has shown confidence in the way he weathers the ups and downs of his career. A lot of these ups and downs have been financial. He is at the top and then he slides. But he knows he will come back. He believes in himself and lets the world know.

What does *The Apprentice* teach us about confidence in the business world? On the show, confidence is comprised of:

A willingness to compete. From the very beginning when a candidate decides to go for the show, they are competing, among hundreds of thousands, for a small number of spaces in the show.

The skills and abilities to perform. A candidate must exhibit the skills and ability to perform or they will hear the words, "You're Fired!"

Comfort in a high profile. If a candidate makes it to the show, they say hello to millions of viewers watching their every move, debating their strategies, cheering them on, shaking their heads in disappointment, and seeing them win and lose.

Creativity and Innovation. A candidate must possess these skills to get noticed. Without them they will not catch the producers or eventually, Donald's attention. They will have to use these skills to win.

The ability to work with others and to lead. Candidates must have the ability to work with others and to lead. They will be part of a team and leader of a team. They will be living together, but striving to be the only one to win.

A desire to win. It is a given that *The Apprentice* candidates have desire to win. The show is designed around winning. Donald Trump wants a winner for his apprentice.

Grace Under Pressure. Candidates and prospective candidates must exhibit grace under pressure. If they do not, they will be out of the running early. Once on the show, the pressure increases. Candidates do not want to crack in front of their teammates, Donald, or the world.

The Apprentice shows us a lot about confidence. How do you develop confidence as a leader? Let's look at some aspects of having confidence. They are: build your self-esteem, the elements of confidence, knowing who you are, and believing in yourself.

Build Your Self-Esteem

The foundation of confidence is your sense of self-esteem. Self-esteem is confidence and satisfaction in oneself. Lack of self-esteem can be disguised in aggression, boisterousness, bravado, cruelty, or anger. But, these traits do not earn trust from others. You must have a sense of self and like what you see to lead well.

How would you rate your sense of self-esteem? What are your core beliefs about yourself? Do you see yourself as a winner or a loser? You must look deeply to answer these questions. The disguises mentioned above can be tricky.

Try this. Make a list about what you were told about yourself as a child. What did people say were your good points and bad? Continue with what people said and what your life experiences told you about yourself though school, in friendships, at work, and at play to the present day. Once you have your list, determine what you like about it.

> What would you add?
> What would you change?
> How does this list jive with what you need to succeed?
> Do you see any clues to your inner beliefs about yourself?

What kind of picture does your list create?
Do you believe you have what it takes to be all you can be?

This inner examination will take you far in your quest for self-esteem. Here are some building blocks you can use to build your self-esteem.

Create small successes and acknowledge them.
Ask others about the good things they see in you.
Choose activities you excel in, whenever you can.
Start working on improving your weak points.
Avoid excessive self-criticism.
Focus instead on acknowledgement and self-improvement.
Set high standards for your performance and meet them.

Self-esteem and personal power go hand in hand. You need both to be a leader.

The Elements of Confidence

What makes up a sense of confidence? Here are several elements we can identify.

Style

Style is your manner of expressing who you are. Consciously or unconsciously you have a certain style.

What comprises your style?
Are you fast or slow?
Are you a competitor or a collaborator?
Are you up front or behind the scenes?
Are you flamboyant or elegant?
What are the attributes of your personal style?

Presence

Presence is how you make yourself known wherever you are. Presence differs from style. It is your way of saying "I am here." Jackie Kennedy had presence whenever she walked into a room. So does Nelson Mandela. As a leader, you need presence. You can develop presence by developing who you are—by knowing yourself and communicating who you are to others. Usually this communication is non-verbal. It is more about how you look, how you speak, what you do, how you interact with others, how you make people feel, and what you stand for.

Identity

Identity is simply who you are. Your identity is comprised of the elements of your life. You are a sister, a brother, a father, a mother, a child, a professional, an artist, a community organizer—a myriad of things. As a leader, how others identify you directly relates to their trust in you. For example, "He has made it up the ranks of our organization. He has what it takes."

Stability

The derivation of stability is from a word meaning to stand. By stability I mean firmness, equilibrium about who you are. You are not like mercury, hard to hold and always in motion. People can count on knowing who you are. There is continuity in your identity.

Sticking Up For Yourself

Donald Trump, on the show, let us know that he thinks this is an essential element of confidence. In the boardroom, in the Planet Hollywood task, Nick saved himself from being fired by giving the reasons why he is a born leader. When Donald fired Kristi, he expressed his disappointment that she did not fight for herself.

Ability to See Your Flaws and Correct Them

If you focus on always defending your actions and do not have the honesty to see your flaws, you will soon wear yourself out. You need the ability to self-correct and grow. If you do this you will get better and better. You will become a stronger leader and your confidence will soar.

Believing in Yourself

Here is the core of confidence. Take all that I've written and wrap it up in this. Believe in yourself, so that others can believe in you. Belief in yourself will help you in many ways. You will know as a challenge presents itself, that you can do it. You will know when you need help and when you can do it alone. You will know that you can make a difference. You will trust your judgment of people and situations. You will end up liking yourself.

Great leaders have to believe in themselves or they will fail. Often leaders find themselves alone, in making decisions or charting a course. They have only themselves to rely on. We often hear the phrase that it is lonely at the top. Many U.S. presidents have poignant reminiscences about the loneliness of power. But often, those memories correspond with their finest hour.

Start today knowing who you are. Believe that you can do what you set your mind to. Exude genuine self-confidence and watch yourself go!

Know Yourself

Knowing yourself is an ongoing, everyday process. Commit to it as an essential ingredient of your leadership style. If *The Apprentice* candidates do not know who they are, they won't make it to first base. They have to submit their profile, sell themselves, and convince the show's producers to give them a chance. They have

---

Assessing your performance as a leader.

Do you know your personal style?

How "aware" are you?

Do you know your values and live by them?

Are you aware of the conditionings and experiences from your earlier life that create boundaries to your leadership potential?

to distinguish themselves from their competition. What are some of the things candidates must know about themselves to compete on *The Apprentice?*

- They can withstand tough competition
- They know how to lead
- They can excel within a group
- They have what it takes to impress Donald
- They can think quickly on their feet
- They can take the heat
- They can have their moves scrutinized
- They can take defeat
- They can distinguish themselves from others
- They can win

Knowing yourself takes commitment and skill. It has to be high on a leader's list of priorities. Do you know yourself? Let's look at what it takes: awareness, assessment, adjustment, and being true.

> "I think Bill is my toughest competition."
> —Amy Henry

Awareness

My husband is a filmmaker. When we first married, he often used the word awareness. He observed the varying levels of awareness that people had, including mine! I was born and raised in New York City. I have spent my career in government and business. When we married I was fast. I got things done. There were miles to go before I would sleep. I lived in the city that never sleeps.

When my husband moved to New York City he noticed a lot of things I had never noticed. He noticed that a high-rise apartment building, under construction, was going to block some of the sun in our kitchen when it was finished. He noticed that living in New York City you had to be "on" as soon as you walked out the door. He loved New York, but was very aware of what it took to live there.

I, in contrast, made it through my life with blinders on. In New York, you must keep your focus. The pace is fast; there is not much room for missteps. She who hesitates is lost. As we lived together, I became more aware. I would notice birds in the sky. I would take in more visual details of the people I was with. And every once in awhile, I slowed down. When I moved to Los Angeles and found myself in a very different environment than New York City, my awareness began to grow. I worked on understanding energy, what point of view I, and others came from, and how I held myself in the world. I began to understand how important awareness is in knowing yourself.

When I work with clients, awareness is frequently our starting point. I ask them to observe situations they are having problems with. I ask them to observe co-workers and situations at work. I ask them to record their observations and tell me what they have learned. In every case, as a client's awareness grows, they know themselves better.

Knowing yourself requires awareness. If you do not know yourself, how can others know you? If you are not aware of others, how can you know where you are?

Assessment

Once you have developed your awareness, how do you assess what you see? Candidates on *The Apprentice* must constantly assess. They must assess themselves against the other candidates. They must assess Donald and his staff and what they are looking for. They must assess the dossier they receive at the start of each task, to ascertain what Donald is looking for and what is needed to win. They must assess themselves against their teammates. They must assess their strengths and weaknesses in the context of each individual task.

To know yourself, you must always be assessing. Why? Because movement is inherent in life. People, conditions, and situations are always changing. You must assess the environment around you and your place in it all. Assessment allows you to adapt, succeed, and improve.

What do you need for a good assessment? You must have objectivity. Defensiveness or skewed judgment has no place in an assessment. You must have clear purpose. You need, before you start, a clear understanding of your goals and what you want to accomplish. You must have insight. You need to develop good analytical skills and understanding of people and situations. Finally, you must have measures. How will you know your assessment is complete? What level of performance do you want to reach?

Developing good assessment skills, getting them to be second nature, will greatly increase your knowledge of self. You manage what you measure. It applies to your life too.

> *"The first step being a real leader is to figure out exactly who you are and be that all the time."*
> —Cathie Black, president of Hearst Magazines quoted in *The Way to the Top*, Donald Trump

Adjustment

When I was growing up, I was often told to "adjust." On one hand, I developed adaptability to many conditions and situations. I could handle a lot. On the other hand, I became too accommodating. Adjustment should be in your own interest. I'm not proposing that you ignore the needs of others. But, when you make adjustments, ensure that they serve you.

On *The Apprentice* the candidates are frequently making adjustments. They adjust to changing conditions. They adjust as part of a team. They adjust their own game plan. They adjust to Donald Trump. He holds the cards for them to win.

Learn to adjust once you assess. Serve your own interest. The word adjust is defined in *Webster's Dictionary* as: to adapt or conform oneself; to achieve mental and behavioral balance between one's own needs and the demands of others. To lead you must have the ability to adjust.

Being True

The adage "To thine own self be true" has survived through time. It is a principle to live by. It assumes that you honor your values. It assumes that you serve your own best interests. That you know yourself and are true to what you know.

How can you do this? Develop some indicators. What does it mean to be true to yourself? It may mean to always be in integrity. It may mean that you speak up for yourself. It may mean you are kind to others. Create a list of the elements of being true to yourself. You each have a unique destiny in life. Only if you are true to yourself, will it manifest. If you are true to the standards and dictates of others, you betray yourself. You are inherently good. Being true to yourself will not hurt yourself or others. You are the best you have. The world wants you. Bring your uniqueness out in your leadership style.

RECAP

Authenticity. Know who you are and accept yourself
Living Out Loud. Enjoy life and fully express who you are
Have confidence. Fully believe you can get the job done.
Know yourself. Acknowledge your strengths and weaknesses and act on them.

EXERCISES

1. Write a description of your authentic self.

2. Identify a way that you can live out loud. Make it something others will see; something that announces that you are alive! Then, in the next month, do it. Assess how it makes you feel. What do you want to do next? What does living out loud mean to you?

3. What does being yourself look like? Pick a candidate on *The Apprentice* and compare and contrast your leadership style with theirs.

CHAPTER FOUR
LESSON THREE: KNOW THE GAME

"IQ may not be the greatest factor in selling lemonade."
—David Gould

David is right. A Ph.D. is not necessary for selling lemonade. What is necessary are location, strategy, sales skills, and a good product. Leaders know the game and the field they are playing in. What does this mean? Outstanding engineering skills won't go very far in selling a penthouse apartment to a prospective buyer. Great marketing skills will not get the building constructed. As a leader, you must be able to understand the environment you are working in—the people, the purpose, the culture, the values, and the rules.

How do you do this? Study and practice. Become an observer in your place of work. Here are several questions to help you begin your process of observation.

Who are the people succeeding in your organization?
What qualities do they have that contribute to their success?
What do you hear from top management about what is important to them?
What is rewarded in your organization?
What does the organization measure in terms of performance?
How would you describe the culture of your organization?

What are the goals of your organization?
How do members of the organization get things done? What are their style and tactics?

At the start of each episode of *The Apprentice*, Donald Trump gives each team a dossier. The dossier provides a description of the task to be completed. It includes the objective and the rules. The teams have what they need to proceed. They know the rules and the goal. If they break the rules, they will not win. If they do not reach the goal, they will lose. The dossier provides a foundation for their strategy.

In your place of work, what are the elements that you can build your strategy on? First, are your performance goals. These goals tell you a lot. They tell you what you will be rewarded for, what expectations you must meet, and what the priorities are. Use your performance goals as the core of your foundation. If you do not meet or exceed them, you are out of the game.

Second is the culture of your organization. What are the norms for behavior and communication? Understand the culture you are working in. As an entrepreneur, you are creating your organization's culture everyday by your style, your decisions, and your priorities. Shortly after the first season of *The Apprentice*, *The Wall Street Journal* (April 20, 2004) had an article on how the Goldman Sachs culture impacted Kwame's performance on the show and helped get him fired. They said Donald Trump passed over Kwame because of his laid-back style and selected a more rah-rah manager instead. Goldman prides itself on its low profile and Donald Trump on the other hand, is legendary for his self-promotion. The article points out that Kwame's style hurt him most when it came to dealing with cast member, Omarosa. She lied to him, costing Kwame points with Donald Trump, who said he should have fired or severely reprimanded her.

Third are your skills. Are your skills a match-up with your performance goals and the culture of your organization? Inventory what skills you rely on to perform well. Are your skills valued by the organization? Do your skills fit what you want to accomplish? Like Kwame, you may have a low-key style, but if your organization wants assertiveness, your foundation may be shaky. What skills do you need to improve your performance?

Now you have a foundation from which to begin knowing the game of work. Here are some tips to help you start.

Be on the Same Page

What does that really mean? It means walking in step, knowing where you are, and not creating a fantasy about the environment you are in. Realistically look at your work environment and understand it and how it operates.

In my work with clients, I have often encountered situations where they do not understand the environment they work in. Initially, they spend a lot of time perplexed and sometimes angry or frustrated by the feedback they receive, the way things are done, and the actions of others. They expend a lot of energy trying to make it right when, in reality, the situation will not change. They are not on the same page as the organization.

I am not speaking of mindless conformity here. Being on the same page involves knowing yourself and your organization and deciding if you can be on the same page. It involves choice. Do you want to be there? Can you succeed there? Are your values aligned with those of the organization?

To answer these questions, let's look at the factors involved in being on the same page in your place of work. They are: immediate environment, other parts of the organization, outside factors, and your life and needs.

Immediate Environment

Your immediate environment consists of the tasks you are expected to perform, the people you work with, and the pressures you face. What is the immediate environment of *The Apprentice*? It is a group of high-performing individuals chosen from hundreds of thousands, who are all there to win. It is close living quarters, high pressure, and tight deadlines. It is a fishbowl with team member performance watched by millions on television as well as by Donald Trump and his staff.

The candidates in the show are all high energy, ambitious, and competitive personalities. They have to team together to win, but at the same time, they are competing against each other for the chance of a lifetime.

Take a moment and imagine yourself as one of *The Apprentice* candidates.

> As you start on the show, how will you get to know your immediate environment and use this knowledge to your advantage?
> How will you align with your environment?
> Will you try to get along?
> Will you watch out for others trying to undermine you?
> Will you reveal your strategy for winning or keep it close?
> Over the course of months you can misstep. How will you handle it when you do?
> As the candidates narrow, how will you interact with your roommates?

Take it a step further. You are also interacting with Donald Trump and his staff within your immediate environment.

> How do you learn about them—their preferences, their standards, and their expectations?
> How do you present yourself to them?
> How do you show them you have what it takes to be The Apprentice?

Now, come back to your life. What are the tasks you are expected to perform at work? Take a look at them and honestly assess how you are doing. If you are doing well—great!

> If not, what can you do to get your tasks done well?
> Do you need to rethink your goals?

Do you need to speak with your boss or customers on their expectations of you?
Do you need a peer review of how you are doing?
Do you need more focus or motivation?
What obstacles lie in your way and how will you deal with them?
Is your workplace chaotic, hindering your ability to perform?

The goal here is to know what your immediate environment is, to function effectively and knowledgeably in it, and to perform well.

In some jobs, the tasks you are expected to perform are not always clear. Workplaces that live from crisis to crisis, disorganized workplaces, downsized workplaces, do not do a good job of defining expectations for performance. If you are in such a situation, what can you do? Observe your workplace keenly. Know its characteristics. Acknowledge its pressures. Take cues from those at higher levels, how do they cope with the immediate environment? Who is successful and why? How do others deal with the pressures? Then, determine how you can function best within this environment.

Your immediate environment is your home base at work. Be on the same page as those around you. Understand how your immediate environment functions and how you can function within it.

Other Parts of the Organization

Other parts of your organization will influence your ability to perform at work. Know these parts of the organization and how they can impact you. For each task given by Donald Trump on *The Apprentice*, numerous factors can influence the team's performance. In the task that involved Trump Taj Mahal Hotel and Casino, teams had to work with various personnel and departments in order to complete their tasks. In the Chrysler-Trump National Golf Classic Tournament, Bill's team had to interact with country club personnel on storing their materials, deciding how long the weather delay would be held, and setting up the dinner. If those interactions did not go well, the team could fail.

What parts of your organization can influence your ability to get a job done? Know them and be on the same page. Take a moment to identify what parts of your organization currently influence your ability to perform. For example, you may work in a technical area and be dependent on computer systems to get your job done. Are you dependent on an internal information services department to approve and service your computer equipment and software? Write down all the parts of the organization that you interact with and/or are dependent on. For each part, assess your interaction with them.

> Is it going well?
> Are there any people or procedures that prevent you from functioning well?
> What works?
> What doesn't work?
> Are there things you can do to improve the situation? How significant is their impact on your performance?

Other parts of your organization are players in your game. Here the same things apply as in your immediate environment. Understand them. Cultivate them, develop and maintain relationships, and build them into your strategy for success. Be on the same page.

Outside Factors

Influences exist outside your organization that can directly impact your ability to perform. These can include a customer base, consumer preferences, economic conditions, political conditions, and even the weather. On *The Apprentice,* each task is affected by outside factors. When renovating and renting apartments, the teams had to consider market conditions and renter preferences and depend on outside construction contractors. When selling Trump Ice, Donald Trump's new brand of bottled spring water, the teams had to deal with restaurants having limited storage space. In the casino, teams had to consider gambler preferences.

How the teams understood and dealt with these outside factors had significant influence on outcome. Know the outside factors that can affect your performance and how to deal effectively with them.

Your Life and Needs

As a professional business coach, I begin with the personal. I want to know my client's values, their dreams, and how they want to live. Once I know this, we can begin to create the work life they desire. Your life and needs matter. You must be on the same page with the organization you are in. In other words, your work must support the way you want to live. When I ran New York City's Hazardous Materials Emergency Response Team, my life and needs were on the same page with my work. I wanted the risk and excitement involved in the emergencies. I wanted the high profile. I could function on call for twenty-four hours a day and find my balance. If my life and needs were about predictability or reasonable work hours, I would not have been on the same page as my work.

The candidates on *The Apprentice* make it clear they want to be there. Their life and needs are on the same page with Donald Trump's design of the competition. They are willing to stand above the crowd of contenders. They are willing to perform and compete. They are self-promoters. They are willing to take months out of their ordinary life to play Donald Trump's game. They like the prize being offered. They have aligned their life and needs with this work.

What kind of life do you want to live? What are your values? How do you want work to fit into your life? Many times people are reluctant to put their needs first. But if you do, you will be taking a major step in finding work you love. When you love your work, you will excel. Let's look at some indicators that your life and needs are not aligned with your work—they are not on the same page.

You are frequently exhausted
Your life is not in balance

You have no life outside your work
To succeed at your work, you cannot honor your values

These are just a few indicators. Some things are worth changing. Others are not. Find work that aligns with your life and needs.

Get on the same page with your work. Understand how the game is played. Put yourself in a game where you can excel.

Don't Waste Your Energy

To win a NASCAR race, a car must have ample fuel or it comes to a stop. Your energy is your fuel. A big part of knowing the game is realizing that you must have the energy to sustain your performance. Otherwise you may succeed for a while, but you will eventually crash and burn.

On *The Apprentice,* a lot is required of the candidates. They have to pull themselves out of their normal environment. This takes energy. They have to compete with a group of people they do not know. This takes energy. They have to leave their work and businesses. This takes energy. They have to move into a communal living situation. This takes energy. And all of this energy is expended before they even begin the competition!

So, consider this: use your energy wisely and you will thrive as a player in the game. Let's discuss three factors in not wasting your energy. They are: really understand the game at work before you play, conserve your energy and use it well, and get out of your conditioning and fantasies and into reality.

> *"There were eight Type-A personalities.*
> *We're not going to be best friends."*
> —Heidi Bressler

Really Understand the Game at Work Before You Play

If you are playing chess, it behooves you to know the difference between a king and a pawn before you begin. So it is with work. I would like to present you with my view of the elements of the high stakes game that Donald Trump plays. You can apply these to any situation you are in. Studying these elements will help you understand the game and use your energy wisely. They are: preparation, power, savvy and style, competition, ambition, and the bottom line.

Preparation

Donald Trump is an excellent negotiator. A key principle of effective negotiation is to be prepared. I imagine before Donald goes into a negotiation he knows the players, how far he is willing to go, has a clear strategy, has determined what his style will be in dealing with the parties involved, and has an exit strategy.

In your work, there are many areas where it behooves you to prepare. Preparing helps you center yourself before you begin a task. Preparing helps you deal with obstacles or surprises. How can you prepare? Here are a few suggestions. Thoroughly know the purpose and goals of a task or meeting before you begin. Give thought to who is involved and, for each person, what expertise they bring and what their agenda may be in this particular situation. Know your agenda and the expertise that you bring. Think out what can happen and how you will respond.

Power

Some people thrive on power, others disdain it. Power is a factor in understanding the game. Do you think Donald Trump understands power? I think so. He knows how to wield it and use it to his advantage. Power does not have to be used in a negative way. It can be used effectively, without hurting others.

To succeed at work you must understand what power is and how to use it. Who do you think is a powerful person? What is it about that person that makes them powerful? Get comfortable with the concept of power. Think about how your work will be different if you understand power and use it effectively.

Savvy and Style

Whether or not it's your cup of tea, Donald Trump has style. He has savvy. This style and savvy are paraded throughout *The Apprentice* as candidates go to his mansion in Florida, fly in the Trump helicopter, and live in Trump Tower. We also see his style in his high standards of performance, concern for the people who work for him, and the value he places on standing up for yourself.

> Do you have a way with people?
> Are you known for your integrity?
> Are you a straight shooter?
> Do you always look on the bright side?
> Do you bring humor into your work?

There are many varieties of savvy and style. You can develop your own. Much of your style is already there. Bring out the best parts of you. Develop your own brand. Use it in your dealings with others. Let it help you succeed.

Competition

Like power, some shy away from competition. But in a game, competition is inevitable. Donald Trump set up *The Apprentice* as a competition leading to the ultimate prize—a two-hundred-fifty-thousand-dollar position in his organization. Accept that you will have to compete to lead and to win. It's part of the game. Prepare yourself as an athlete does—get yourself in good form, know the rules, know your advantage, study your opponents, and play to win.

Ambition

Donald Trump has ambition. His beginnings were humble compared to where he is today. He has high ambition for *The Apprentice.* He did not set out to create a second-class show. What do you aspire to? Factor your aspirations into the way you play the game. Always have them in mind. Ambition allows you to recognize the path that will take you where you want to go.

The Bottom Line

Donald Trump focuses on the bottom line. Many of us play the game absorbed in the details. You may get caught in emotions, personalities, or individual challenges. Always keep your eye on the bottom line. Know what it is and let it guide you in playing the game. The bottom line consists of the ultimate goal. What are you working to accomplish? Is the bottom line keeping to a certain cost, getting a client or customer on board, or achieving an end? Define it and don't let it leave your sight.

If you really understand the game you are playing, you will direct your energy in a focused manner. You will not waste your energy. Your moves will make sense and will get you where you want to go.

Conserve Your Energy; Use it Well

Directing your energy to serve you in playing the game is not the whole story. You also need to conserve your energy and use it well. You need endurance and you need to be able to run when you have to. You may be a sprinter or a long distance runner. Whatever you are, understand that you won't make it in the game if you do not understand how to manage your energy level. Let's look at some factors in using your energy. They are: energy drains, energy promoters, and being in the flow.

Energy Drains

Do you wonder where your time goes? What are the energy drains that keep you from doing what you want? Energy drains are the situations, people, or things that keep you from moving forward. On *The Apprentice*, there are examples of

Things that can drain your energy:

Wasting time or using time inefficiently

Unnecessary conflict

Distraction

Worry

Relationships that only "take" from you

Doing too many things

Getting too involved in others' lives

energy drains. One clear energy drain is personality conflicts. When candidates do not get along, their conflicts and tensions drain the energy of those involved, as well as the group. Another example is when a team is not on the same page in completing a task. The effort required to get on the same page and work in sync, could be spent better elsewhere.

As you come to the end of a day, do you find yourself exhausted, unable to do another thing? Are you irritable with people? The underlying reason for being in this state may not be the number of things you do. It may be that the stresses, frustrations, and pressures you experience drain your energy to a point where you can do no more.

An essential element of using your energy wisely is to eliminate the energy drains that rob you of your time, your dreams, and your happiness. Energy drains are counterproductive forces in your life.

You can start identifying the energy drains in your life through observation. Look at the situations that create stress and keep you from doing the things that are important to you. Look carefully at the price you are paying by allowing these energy drains to affect your life.

> **Things that can give you energy**
>
> successes at work
>
> sharpening your skills
>
> physical exercise
>
> time with family/friends
>
> having fun
>
> reading a good book,
>
> playing a team sport
>
> having some time just for you.

Energy Promoters

Once you have identified the energy drains in your life, set out to eliminate them. Begin to replace them with things that promote your energy. Energy promoters give you energy. They make you feel good. They give you what you need to move forward. Make room for these things in your life. You will see your life change in wonderful ways when you say goodbye to energy drains and focus on the things that build your energy.

Being in the Flow

Do you flow with life? Do you fight where life takes you or accept where you are? You know it is easier to flow downstream than to paddle upstream. So it is with life. Flowing with life serves your best interest. Flowing is a better use of your energy than resisting. But, how do you flow with life? It is not an easy concept to master. Often, humans equate control of our circumstances with security and happiness. Flow involves, to some extent, letting go of control.

What is flow as it applies to your life? Flow is a sense of ease. It is the ability to adapt to what happens and the presence of mind to make choices in your best interest. Flow is about acceptance of what life brings you. Flow is about rolling with life instead of resisting it. Flow is smooth, uninterrupted movement.

Get Out of Your Conditionings and Fantasies and Into Reality

If you want to use your energy well, know what your realities are. On *The Apprentice* this is essential. If a candidate comes into the competition thinking the game is just like their game at home, watch out. They won't make it. The game is played in New York City, a city like no other, and Donald Trump is writing the rules.

By conditionings, I am referring to a number of things. Conditionings include the things you learned as a child that do not serve your present situation. The fears you carry with you or bad habits you formed. For example, if you had a critical parent whose approval you always sought, you may bring that need for approval into your workplace.

By fantasies, I mean just that—unrealistic or improbable notions. For example, believing you will compete on *The Apprentice* and be so good, you will get Donald Trump's job and he'll be out. A big fantasy!

If you eliminate energy drains, replace them with energy promoters, and get out of your conditionings and fantasies, you will see a huge increase in your energy level. You will be able to use your energy to know the game and play it well.

Know Where You Fit In

The Apprentice candidates know where they fit in. They have been chosen from many to compete for a position in the Trump organization. They know they are there because of their business acumen, success in their field, drive, and ambition. They know they have to complete tasks, lead, perform effectively, and win. The game board is set. Donald Trump has chosen them because they are a good fit for what he wants to do—find the right person for his organization.

Knowing where you fit in at work is about both how you fit into your organization and how your organization fits with you. Think of your organization as a jigsaw puzzle. How do you fit into the puzzle? Where are you placed? "Fit" is about harmony, being suitable, and being in accord. In knowing the game, it is essential that you fit into the game, that you can be a player, and that you can play.

> *"Some people have a sense of the market and some people don't."*
> —Donald Trump, *The Art of the Deal*

What is a Fit?

There are many levels operating on *The Apprentice*. It is clear that all candidates on the show are a fit to compete for a place in the Trump organization. But they also have to fit with the other candidates in order to compete together as a team. They have to live together. Then, they have to fit with Donald Trump and his organization.

Each candidate on *The Apprentice* has to assess this fit for themselves. Once they have, they can create an effective playing strategy. Some candidates may decide they are not a fit with the other candidates. They may not trust them or they may prefer operating on their own. They know, however, their success depends on working as a team, so they adjust accordingly. Other candidates may decide to play on the fringes. Others may decide that it is only Donald Trump who matters and their focus is how they perform in the boardroom. Each candidate assesses how and where they fit in. You can use this analysis in assessing whether your work is a fit for you.

How do you fit into your workplace or marketplace?

If you are an entrepreneur, where is your place within your field?

Is there a need for your services?

Who are your customers?

If you are in an organization, what is your contribution to the organization?

Who depends on you and whom do you depend on?

Are there areas where there is not a fit?

If so, what is going on? Is it something you can remedy?

Is the lack of fit going to adversely affect your performance?

You have to be a good fit with your work. You must contribute to your organization's success and well-being and it must contribute to yours.

Know Who You Are

It is obvious on *The Apprentice* that each candidate has a good sense of who they are. No surprise that they have succeeded in life. They each know how to play to their strengths and minimize their weaknesses. They know how to self-promote to get chosen for the show. They are excellent in presenting themselves as winners who can do the job. They make themselves very attractive to Donald Trump and his organization.

What do you know about yourself? First, assess your strengths. What strengths do you bring to your work? Are you using your strengths to get ahead? Sometimes your strengths can be out of sync with the work you are doing. Have you found that the work you do is unappreciated? Sometimes, such lack of appreciation is a result of a bad fit. What do I mean by that? If your strengths do not meet the need that exists, the job cannot get done well. Make sure that the strengths you have are a good fit with the work you do.

Next, assess your weaknesses in much the same way. Where do your weaknesses lie? Are your weaknesses hindering your performance? We all have weaknesses. The key here is to make sure that the areas you are weak in are not critical to getting your job done. You can improve on your weaknesses once you identify them. If you identify a weakness, decide what you need to improve. Do you need training? Do you need a mentor? Do you need to study? You can also minimize the affect your weaknesses have by choosing work that plays to your strengths.

It does not serve you to try to hide who you are. Nor does it serve you to pretend you are something you are not. Be genuine. Know who you are and you will find the right fit.

Know the Playing Field

I referred earlier to knowing the game you are in, looking at the goals you are given, the culture you are in, and where your skills lie. You must understand your immediate environment, other parts of your organization, and outside factors that affect your work. Now let's go deeper and look at the playing field you are on.

On *The Apprentice,* the basics of the game are clear. As a candidate you will compete on a team to beat another team in a particular task. At the end, if you make it, you'll be in a one-on-one competition to win. But, to succeed, there are a lot more things the candidates must know. They must know what Donald Trump and his staff are looking for. They must know the strengths and weaknesses of the other candidates. They must learn as much as they can, within the time given, about the critical factors involved in each task.

In your work, deepening your knowledge of the playing field can involve looking at who matters, how you are measured, who defines the rules of the game, keeping the end result in mind.

Who Matters

Begin by identifying the critical players on your playing field.

Who are the people who can have the most impact on your success or failure?

Look at your current relationship with each of them.

How is your communication with each one?
What do they think of you?
What do you think of them?
Which are your strongest relationships, i.e. the ones that will help you succeed?
Which are your weakest relationships?
For your weaker relationships, what can you do to improve them?
If you are unable to improve them, can you function within the situation or do you have to change something?

To know your playing field, know who matters.

How You Are Measured

On *The Apprentice*, candidates are very clear on what their measures are. The dossier for each task presents the objective and the rules. They know what they have to do to win. They know ultimately that Donald Trump will decide who will best serve his organization. As an entrepreneur, you determine the measures among a myriad of factors such as market and competition. In a workplace you are often given your measures. Sometimes in a workplace, measures may exist on paper, but may not fully answer the question of how you are measured. In that case, you have to go beyond the paper to know how you are measured. How can you do this? In some cases you may be able to directly ask your supervisors what they are looking for. You can observe what you are rewarded for and when your work is considered deficient. Knowing how you are measured is important to your knowledge of the playing field.

Who Defines the Rules of the Game

There are rules on every playing field. Know who defines the rules on yours. Sometimes, the answer is not obvious. The chief of your organization may set the vision and direction of the organization, but when it comes to day-to-day operations, another person may define the rules. You need to know who has say over your success or failure in the organization. This is also true concerning outside factors, such as the customers you interact with. Rules are made by anyone who has a say on your performance. Once you know who defines the rules, you can listen and know what the rules really are.

Keep the End Result in Mind

The purpose of a game is to win. Always keep the end result in mind. If you get lost in details or short-term moves, you could lose sight of the end point.

The end point can be both what you want to achieve and what your organization wants you to achieve. Define your end point and always keep it in mind.

Understanding How it Works

The Apprentice candidates come to the show with a good idea of how the business world works. They could not have succeeded in the world without this knowledge. Donald Trump is looking for people who have this understanding. To know where you fit in, you must understand how the game is really played. Here are a few things to consider. They are integral parts of how the game is played, but are not always visible on the surface. They are: power, hidden rules, and energy.

Power

Power shows up, once again, in knowing how the game is played. Your understanding and use of power is critical to knowing where you fit in. If you do not understand power, you are not on the playing field. What is power? Power is your ability to get what you want. Donald Trump has power. He can get a building built and he can sell apartments in it at top dollar. He gets what he wants in a challenging and tough business world.

What can power get you on your playing field? For you, power may mean being able to lead a team effectively to get the job done. It may mean having influence in your organization, so that your views are heard. It may mean that you have the skills the organization needs to accomplish their goals. Power is everywhere. Some know how to use it, some don't. If you are going to understand the game, you must know how to have and use power.

> *"Money was never a big motivator for me except as a way to keep score. The real excitement is playing the game."*
> —Donald Trump, *The Art of the Deal*

Hidden Rules

In the game of work, there are always hidden rules. You have to be astute to find them. You cannot play effectively without knowing them. In many workplaces, there is a chess game being played underneath the surface game. What is this chess game? It is directly linked to how players use and wield their power.

In one organization I worked in, it was a big revelation for me to discover the existence of these hidden rules. I realized I was playing a very different game than my superiors. I was focused on results and quality. I was a producer, I cultivated long-term client relationships, and I produced high quality work. Although I was acknowledged and well compensated for my work, the promotion I had been promised did not come. As I looked deeper, I found the hidden rules of the game that I had been oblivious to. In that game, the first rule was to follow the boss' personal agenda. It was not about the goals of the organization, but about stroking his ego and playing what he wanted to play. Although I was recognized as a performer, I would not reach the inner circle because they were playing by rules I didn't even know.

You can find these rules by observing how power is used in your organization. Start by observing the people who have power. Look at their body language, how they get what they want, how they play the game, and what they reward in others. As you look at each person, think of him or her as a player in a chess game, of how they make their moves. This will help you to identify the hidden rules of the game you are in.

Energy

To understand energy in the workplace is to know the forces that underlie how people act and interact. Energy is the effect you experience from individuals you encounter and the effect they experience from you. At work, there are many types of "energy." What do I mean by energy? Energy is a much-used word. *Webster's Dictionary* defines energy as "the capacity of acting or being active." *American Heritage Dictionary* defines energy as "the work a physical system is capable of doing in changing from its actual state to a specified reference state."

Energy, in the context of the workplace, can be an elusive concept to understand. It takes focus and a willingness to go beyond surface appearances. Energy is always there. We give out energy and are affected by the energy others give out daily in our work and life situations. We can use our energy to affect another person. Energy is unseen, but it is tangible-we feel it. Think of how you feel when someone is angry with you. That is energy—you are experiencing the energy of that person. Energy is not emotion—sadness, happiness, or otherwise—it is an interaction, an exchange. Energy is an underlying force field that is often disregarded, but when understood, is a gateway to power, both the positive and negative forms of power.

Learn to Play

Candidates for *The Apprentice* have to jump right in and learn to play. Although they know Donald Trump's expectations, they do not know what tasks they will be given, nor what the players they will be both teaming with, and competing against at the same time. They do not have much time to learn to play, but their success depends on it.

Set your goal, right now, not only to learn the game, but also to become expert at it. This entails having focus and intent and learning everything you can while still performing at your work. Become a student of the game. Begin with observation. There is no better way to know something then to observe it. Make it fun. Start with observing who wins in your workplace. Pretend you are an eagle flying high above your workplace.

What do you see?
How are people interacting?
What is getting done?
What are the results achieved?
From this eagle's eye view of your workplace, what did you learn?

Here are some varied examples of things you could find.
Players who sell the most widgets end up winning
Players who "play up" to their superiors end up winning
Players who do what they are told end up winning
People who thrive well in chaos and crisis end up winning
Integrity is not rewarded in your organization
Players with the highest profile end up winning
Loyal players end up winning

You can also observe how things get done in your organization.
What methods are most effective and get results?
What methods don't work?
Observe what creates problems in your organization.
Is assertiveness or aggression frowned upon?
Does the squeaky wheel get the grease?
Observe how problems are handled.
Are they addressed directly?
Are they swept under the rug?
Are people fired when they do not perform?
Is the organization endlessly reorganizing to avoid taking action?

Once you have observed the game for a while and have a good sense of how it is played, start playing in it. Try out some strategies at winning. Do it quietly. Do not reveal to others what you are doing. If your organization rewards assertiveness, try taking an assertive stand in a meeting. See what reaction you get. If your organization rewards innovation, develop some innovative ideas and present them. See what winning ways of playing the game fit with you. After you test them out, pick the best ones and start doing them. Bring winning ways into your work, so that you can be a winner.

One important element in being expert at the game is to learn to respond, not react. In doing this, do not let others determine whether you win or lose. Control your destiny. Good and bad will both happen. But, you can choose how you will respond in each situation. You can pick the response that is in your best interest. If you react, you are allowing others to define your playing field.

As you learn to play, you will get good at the game. Just knowing the game exists gives you a big advantage. Enjoy the game and learn what it takes to win.

RECAP

Be on the same page. Understand how the game is played in your place of work.
Don't waste your energy. Play the game you're in, not another one.
Know where you fit in. Maximize your strengths. Know your weaknesses.
Learn to play. Get good at the game and win.

EXERCISES

1. What are the rules, both stated and unstated, in your place of work? Write them down as you would list the rules of a game.

2. Create a description of your work that fits into a particular sport, or a game like chess. For example, Acme Manufacturing Co. as a football game. Describe the players, rules, strategies, and goals in terms of football.

3. Identify three energy drains you want to eliminate. (If you cannot identify them now, spend a day of "observation" to discover them.) Write them down on a piece of paper. For each energy drain, write down one thing you will do in the next week to begin to eliminate it.

CHAPTER FIVE
LESSON FOUR: MAINTAIN BALANCE

"Heidi, do you need to leave?" —Donald Trump

During the first season of *The Apprentice,* Heidi Bressler received a phone call informing her that her mother was seriously ill. Donald Trump called Heidi into the boardroom to privately express his concern and ask Heidi if she needed to leave. Heidi answered that with the support of her family, she had decided to stay. From the time she received this news, Heidi showed an impressive ability to maintain her balance. Amidst her concern for her mother, she was competing for a top prize in front of millions of people. She did it well.

A leader must learn to maintain balance or they will soon burn out or lose the support of people around them. You have seen leaders who run around at breakneck speed, and seem to spend much more time getting things done than is really necessary. And there are the leaders who bring their anger and frustration to work. Or, a leader that burns out, paying for it with poor health and fatigue. Many times the cause is that their life is out of balance. They do not have the equilibrium that is needed to act from a centered place. They are not very good at maintaining balance.

Balance is a state of centering among the many demands of your life. Maintaining balance allows you to function effectively and productively. The ability to choose is an essential element of balance. It is the ability to say yes, I will have this in my life, or no, I will let go of this. You must be able to choose powerfully and clearly what the components of your life will be. What are the elements of your life? In my training at the Coaches Training Institute, we were given a balance wheel that was divided into eight areas: friends and family, fun and recreation, career, money, physical environment, personal growth, health, and romance. How is your life balanced among these areas?

Source: The Coaches Training Institute, www.thecoaches.com

As you choose what balance looks like in your life, there are no hard and fast rules. What is important is that you meet your basic needs and create a life that works well for you. One person may put a high priority on family life. Another may focus on career. Another may focus on health, having just recovered from a serious illness. To begin assessing what balance is for you, identify the priorities in your life. Then, look realistically at what is possible. Assess what balance is for you. Here are some questions to ask yourself.

What Must Get Done in My Life?

If you need to earn a living, a significant amount of your time may have to go to this area of your life. Look at the time required for what must get done. How much of your time must you give to these things?

What is My Passion?

What do you need in your life to live it fully?

What areas of the wheel must you give time to in order to express your passion?

Where Do I Want My Life to Be?

Which areas of the wheel do you want to give time to that you are not now?

In what proportion?

Look at your present reality and think about getting from there to where you want to be.

What's Happening Now?

How does your current life look on the balance wheel?

Is it working?

Are you centered?

Where Do I Want to Be?

Draw a new balance wheel that allocates your time proportionately to achieve the level of balance you desire. Each area of the wheel will have a size relative to the time you will give it. Is it realistic? Can you get yourself there? What needs to happen to achieve this level of balance?

To become an effective leader, bring your life into balance. Here are some things to focus on as you work to achieve balance.

Acknowledge All Parts of Yourself

To be in balance there must be harmony. On a wheel, all spokes are aligned and in motion. To achieve balance in your life, start with an awareness of the physical, mental, emotional, and spiritual aspects of your life. All these things are part of bringing your life into balance.

To compete and excel, *The Apprentice* candidates need to be aware of their physical, mental, emotional and spiritual needs. They need physical stamina to keep up with the pace of tasks given to them. Often, they have only one day to perform. They need a keen mind to meet the challenges they face, to assess their competition, and to design their strategy to win. They need balanced emotions. Misusing their emotions can create missteps and complications that will take time to deal with. They need a spiritual foundation to endure the many demands on them and excel.

A tool that I have found very helpful in achieving balance is another wheel. In this wheel, the south is your physical life, the west your emotional life, the north your spiritual life, and the east your mental life. The goal is to sit in the center of the wheel, balanced among these four aspects.

Wheel for Balance

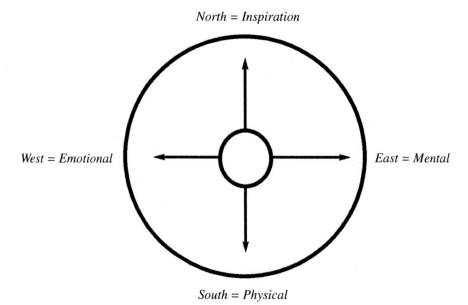

I observe where on the wheel I am focusing my attention and time. Am I balanced? In one period of my life I began journaling each day where I was living on the wheel. I found I was living primarily in the west—my emotions, and south—the physical. I was in a demanding circumstance. I had a lot to accomplish, which brought me to the south. I also was dealing in a challenging personal situation at work, which was getting the better of me. I was not interacting effectively nor was I holding my power in the situation. I was spending a lot of my time in negative emotions of anger and frustration. Once I realized what was happening, I used the wheel as my guide. To be centered, I had to spend more time in the north and east. In the north, I sought spiritual support to help get me through the difficult personal interaction. In the east I moved my focus more to my mind. It got me out of my emotions and also helped me use my intellect to decide how I would handle the challenges. It worked! I regained my equilibrium and improved the situation. Coming more from my center, I gained power and knew what to do.

To maintain balance, acknowledge all parts of yourself. Here are some questions to get you started. They are: What are your needs? What are you neglecting? Where is your center?

> *"We're looking at Kwame under pressure*
> *and he seems to be cracking a little bit."*
> —Mark Brown, CEO Trump Taj Mahal Hotel and Casino

What Are Your Needs?

To answer this question, let's use the wheel developed by the Coaches Training Institute, which I mentioned earlier in this chapter. Assess in each of the eight areas of the wheel, what your needs are.

Physical Environment

Look at what kind of environment you need to live in to maintain balance. This encompasses the town or area you live in, your home and its physical surroundings, your neighbors, and inside your home including its design, the people and animals you share it with, and the level of activity that exists there.

Career

Look at your work life and what you need to maintain balance. This encompasses your level of fulfillment in what you do, your passion, the people you work with, the amount of time you spend working, emotions you have regarding your work, and the level of flexibility available in your work.

Money

Look at the financial state you are in, how it affects your balance, and what you need to maintain a balanced life. This encompasses your current financial situation, any pressures you feel, what you need financially to reach the goals you have in life, what people in your life depend on your financial support, and how you feel about money.

Health

Look at the current state of your health and what you need to maintain balance. This encompasses your energy level, any medical problems that alter your ability to do things, your physical fitness, and how well you take care of your physical needs.

Friends and Family

Look at the role your friends and family play in your ability to maintain balance. This encompasses the level of support and comfort you receive from them, the relationships you have that drain you and the ones that fuel you, the time you desire to have with family and friends, and what you give to your relationships.

Romance

Look at the role of romance in your current life and what you need to maintain balance. This encompasses partnership, love, dating, marriage, and the excitement and fulfillment that come with romance.

Personal Growth

Look at your own desire to seek knowledge and other forms of spiritual fulfillment and what level you need to maintain balance. This encompasses your sense of inquisitiveness about life, your spiritual foundation, self-improvement, and what you are searching for.

Fun and Recreation

Look at how much fun you have in life and its role in your ability to maintain balance. This encompasses what you do for fun, whether fun helps you relieve stress, and how much you enjoy your life.

What Are You Neglecting?

If the candidates on *The Apprentice* neglect any aspect of a task, their neglect could cause them to be fired. If you neglect an aspect of your life that contributes to your sense of balance, you will experience repercussions. You can go for a long time neglecting some things, but not forever. As you look at the level of balance in your life, take some time to identify if there are any parts of your life that you are neglecting. In addition to vital aspects, look at the things you need in your life to feel fulfilled. You may need frequent vacations or time to pursue a hobby. These things are also important to your sense of balance and should not be neglected.

A common example is neglecting your health. If you work long hours, get insufficient sleep, and neglect your physical needs, your body can keep up for awhile. But, at some point you will see indicators that something is amiss. You may experience fatigue. Your emotions may get the better of you because you are tired. You may start being irritable with those around you. Your immune system may weaken, resulting in more colds or other illnesses. Eventually, if you do not restore balance, the signs will get bigger. You may experience more illness. Your stress level could get dangerously high. What starts as a wobble, may result in serious health problems.

The impact of neglecting parts of your life that are vital to your sense of balance can be significant. To perform well, you must maintain a certain level of equilibrium. If your sense of balance is disrupted in one area of your life, it will affect other areas. When you are out of balance, you can experience a range of symptoms such as: inability to concentrate, stress, or making mistakes, to illness, breakdown of relationships, or serious accidents.

Learn to recognize the indicators that your life is out of balance. They vary for each of us. Most likely you are neglecting something. When you see an indicator, do what you need to do to correct the situation. Sometimes, you may not have the opportunity to correct it right away. You can start with small things leading up to bigger corrective measures.

When I was working as an environmental consultant, I managed a project that meant millions of dollars to our client. By the second month, we had a large team and were working seven days a week. I knew I had to keep that pace to get the project completed. To stay in balance, at least three days a week I took time at lunch to go to the gym. I made sure I got eight hours sleep a night. If I was very tired at work and no major deadline was looming, I took a few hours off. I told my husband not to expect to see me and he was okay with that. It would be for a limited time.

We completed the project successfully. I promised my husband we would take a long weekend away for the upcoming holiday. As the holiday approached, my boss told me I had to stay to finish a proposal. I told him I would work till the holiday started, but that after all the hours I put in, I could not give this time up. I told him he and others could finish it without me. It was a risk, but I knew that time away was essential to my sense of balance. It all worked out fine. We won the job with our proposal. It was a big lesson for me. I could draw the line and take care of myself. I was able to restore balance.

When you lose your sense of balance and then regain it, take some time to examine what has happened. Look at how you got out of balance, what you were neglecting, what the indicators were, how quickly you noticed the indicators, how it affected you, and what you did to regain balance. This examination will help you develop a keen awareness of when you are neglecting something that is essential to your sense of balance.

Where is Your Center?

You see the wheel metaphor used frequently in discussions of life balance. In asking where your center is, we can use it again. In a wheel, the spokes move out from a center point. In your life, what is that center point? For humans, center is a point of equilibrium. Your center can be your values, or a silent place, or your religious faith. It can be many things. Your center is a place to move out into the world from and to return to for replenishment. It is a steady point, a place that holds you together. Give some thought to where your center point lies.

The Ability to Choose

The ability to choose is an essential element of balance. It is the ability to say yes, I will have this in my life or, no, I will let go of this. You must be able to choose powerfully and clearly what the components of your life will be. *The Apprentice* is full of choices: candidates must be chosen, teams must choose how to pursue a project, there are choices to make within projects, serious choices must be made by the losing project manager in the boardroom—who will he or she bring back to face Donald, and ultimately, Donald must choose who is fired and who is hired.

In my coaching, I have found that many clients narrow the options available to them in situations. I call it "putting blinders on." As they face a choice, they immediately limit their choices. For example, if they are looking for a new job. They might want to change fields. They place an immediate limit on themselves and say, "Because I am changing fields I know I have to take a salary cut." Or, they say, "I can't go into that field because I'll never get the salary I need," or "I do not have the skills they want." These things may be true, but at least give yourself the time to check out your assumptions. You never know what you will find. Give yourself the full range of options as you start.

I'm not sure why people limit their choices. Perhaps it is due to prior conditionings, beliefs, or perceptions they have about something. But, nothing is absolute in our world. Things can change. What if Donald Trump had said, "I'll never get anyone to pay millions of dollars for my apartments?"

Where is it written that you do not have a full range of choices available to you? You do. Some choices you make may take more time and effort to realize. Some may turn out to be unattainable. But, you owe it to yourself to give all your choices fair consideration. As you approach a decision, identify all choices available to you. Do not limit them. As you look at each choice available, identify how you would pursue that choice. What needs to be in place? What do you need to do? Consider if this choice is what you really want and the impacts this choice will have on your life and those around you.

Choice is your right. No one or nothing can take that away from you. Considering your full range of choices opens the world to you. It allows you to breathe. It honors who you are and what you can become. With an open mind, you have a much better chance of realizing your dreams.

What limits do you place on your ability to choose? Take a look at them; then begin to let them go. The next time you have a choice to make, give full range to your options. Exaggerate a bit. Shoot for the moon. If you are thinking of starting a business, consider some far out choices. Perhaps you will structure the business to franchise in three years. Imagine that venture capital will be easy to come by because your idea is so good. Starting with all options helps you in determining what is right for you. Self-imposed limits do not serve you. They take away your possibilities.

Here are some ways you can use your ability to choose to maintain balance in your life. They are: what does balance look like for you, eliminate tolerations, discriminate, and exercise choice.

What Does Balance Look Like For You?

Balance is an individual thing. What balance looks like for someone else, can be very different than what balance looks like for you. Some people can spend long hours working and still maintain balance. Work gives them energy, rather than taking it away. Some people must have solitude to maintain their balance. Some may need time with family and friends. For each person, there is a unique formula for balance. Understand what balance looks like for you.

When Heidi found out her Mom was sick, she decided, with the support of her family, she would continue on the show. It had to be difficult, but she did it. Another person may have decided to leave the show. The strain would have been too much.

What does balance look like for you? It may take some time and experimenting for you to answer this question. A tool I use with clients may help you do this. For a week, they monitor how they use the one hundred sixty-eight hours in their week, including sleeping, eating, and other activities. Once they do this they see what the balance of their life was for that week. Then we look together at whether that balance works for them and if they want to make adjustments. If they do, we eliminate things in order to make room for others. Because one hundred sixty-eight hours are finite, this is not always easy for them to do. They end up wanting a lot more hours in the day! But, by persisting and making choices, my clients find what balance looks like for them.

In order to maintain balance, you must know what it looks like for you. Balance is not built on fantasies, such as I want to do everything and do it now. Balance involves choice, focus, and realism. Balance is a wheel. If it is not aligned it will not spin. Align yourself in balance and your life will move forward.

> *"Pick a career that you really love, and then you will love what you do. And if you love what you do, you'll be successful!"*
> —Laurie Scala, president of Clean Water Technologies, Inc. quoted in *The Way to the Top*, Donald Trump

Eliminate Tolerations

A central principle in coaching is that eliminating the tolerations in your life will lead you to balance and fulfillment. Tolerations are aspects of our lives that slowly and quietly drain our energy and keep us from pursuing our dreams. What do I mean by tolerations? I mean the things that you allow to exist in your life that do not serve you. For example: the extra twenty pounds that keep you feeling sluggish, the friend who consistently crosses your boundaries, no matter what you tell them, the coworker who creates great stress by their frequent outbursts of anger, or the knowledge that you are underpaid for the work you do. When you eliminate your tolerations, you simultaneously reduce your stress and make room for new things to come into your life. Eliminating tolerations will help you maintain balance in your life.

Do you see examples of tolerations on *The Apprentice*? Are team members tolerating lazy or obnoxious behavior from another team member? Is a candidate accepting something less than excellence in their own performance? If you identify a toleration on the show, observe it. Look at the effects that toleration is having. If the toleration were not accepted, what would result? Where will things go if the toleration continues?

What are you tolerating? Do you want to eliminate the tolerations in your life? Start by identifying what they are. Create a list of the tolerations in your life. Include them all. Post the list as a reminder that these are things you want to eliminate in your life. Then one by one, eliminate them. If they involve other people, start in a compassionate way. Tell them what you would like to change and why you feel that way. Ask them if they will support you in changing the situation. If the toleration is about you, get moving and address it. Be kind to yourself, but set a strong intent to change. Make a commitment not to allow new tolerations in your life. A life without tolerations is a free life. It is within your power to achieve.

Discriminate

Discrimination is the essence of balance. As our world grows more complex, the ability to discriminate becomes more and more important, if you are to maintain a sense of balance and harmony in your life. It is important that you be able to say no, to exclude those things that no longer serve you.

Sometimes people resist discriminating. You may not like to make choices. You may not want to say no to someone. You may wish you could have all of it. In reality, if you do not discriminate how much can you really have? There is not enough time and space to have absolutely everything. Allow yourself to let go of things in your life that do not serve you. Sometimes, this may involve hard choices. But, make them. You may find that by saying no now, you make it possible to say yes later.

Let's say you are running a new business. It is very demanding of your time. You want a vacation, but if you leave for two weeks, the business could falter. You decide to stay home and take a day off. A year later, your business is thriving, you have a manager you can rely on and you take your vacation.

You can have quite a lot, if you discriminate. I bet Donald Trump is skilled at discriminating. How could he manage his businesses if he did not say no to some things? My guess is he says no to what he considers low-return pursuits, wasting his time, or getting into no-win battles with other business people or government regulators. He has a lot he wants to do. He needs time to accomplish his ambitions.

You must be able to choose powerfully and clearly what the components of your life will be. Otherwise, you will miss the magnificent moments in your life because you are juggling too many balls in the air. Discrimination is proactive rather than reactive. Discrimination implies responsibility; that you are taking charge of your life and choosing the life you want. It makes the difference between having a life you can celebrate and tolerating whatever circumstances get dumped on you.

Exercise Choice

I'm sure it is clear to you by now that I consider choice a key ingredient of balance. To maintain balance, you must exercise choice. Make choice an active verb in your life. Choice implies action. Believe that you deserve a good life and can choose what you want it to be. Be on the lookout for hidden beliefs or conditionings that close off options. Give yourself free reign to exercise choice.

Make responsible choices. Free reign does not give you permission to hurt yourself or others. When a choice is before you, fully explore your options. Consider what is in your best interest. Know the consequences, good and bad, of each option. Develop a system of choice making that works for you. Your system could include ways to identify all of your options, questions to ask yourself about each option, a way to analyze the impacts each choice will have, a way to use your values as a benchmark for making your choice, or a group of people you can talk with as you make your choice.

Never limit your options without good reason. Create a keen awareness of beliefs or conditionings that sabotage your freedom of choice. Limits are not bad in themselves. They can be based on real conditions you cannot change, your own preferences, the needs of people who matter to you, or other matters that have priority. Allow limits only if they serve your own interests.

As you begin to make choices, observe them and yourself. Are things changing in your life now that you are exercising choice? How are you feeling about the choices you are making? What's different from how you used to make choices? How is your life going? Has exercising choice had an impact? Has exercising your ability to choose helped you maintain balance? Think of what your answers to these questions would be if you were selected as a candidate for *The Apprentice*? Run through possible answers just for fun.

At some point, review the impacts of the choices you make and let them inform your future. What do these impacts tell you about how you can make choices in the future? Do any choices stand out as building blocks for your future? What are the positive and negative lessons learned from exercising your freedom of choice?

A Strong Foundation

To achieve balance, you must have a strong foundation for your life. This means taking steps to create a life that supports your basic needs. It means self-care and acknowledging that only with a strong foundation can you be of service to yourself and others. Here again, we return to the physical, emotional, spiritual, and mental aspects of your life. Each aspect needs to rest on a secure foundation.

How do you do this? You go back to fundamentals. It is a simple, but not an easy process. You acknowledge your needs in each aspect of your life. You identify what you can do to meet those needs. Let's look at each aspect and what constitutes a strong foundation. For each person, there will be differences, but the following will give you a sense of how to begin.

Building a Physical Foundation

A physical foundation starts with your body—health, nutrition, fitness, and wellness. From there it moves to how you live physically in the world—home, work, and play. You begin by assessing where you want your life to be on a physical level. Here are some things to look at.

> What is the present state of your health?
> Are you as healthy as you want to be?
> What are your eating habits?
> Do you want to change them?
> How much do you exercise?
> Are you as fit as you want to be?
> How is your physical environment at home?
> Does it nurture you?
> Does it cause you stress?
> Is there anything about it that you want to change?
> How is your work life?
> Are you happy in it?
> How does your work life affect your overall being?

How much fun do you have?
How do you play?
Could you use more fun in your life?

Once you assess the physical aspects of your life, can you say your physical life is where you want it to be? If it is, congratulations. You can move on to the emotional aspects of your life. If your physical life is not where you want it to be, identify what you want to change about it. Once you have identified what you want to change, set out to do it. This is the beginning of building your physical foundation.

Building an Emotional Foundation

Your emotional foundation touches many aspects of your life. Emotions are like winds that move through your life affecting all that you do. How do you begin setting your emotional foundation? You look at your relationships, your feelings, how you express or do not express your emotions, and at the role emotions play in your life. Here are some things to look at.

Do I express my emotions freely or do I hold them in?
What happened in my childhood when I expressed emotions?
How did that affect what I do today?
How are the relationships in my life?
Do they nurture me?
Or, do they create stress?
Am I an emotional person?
How do my emotions influence my personality and how I walk in the world?
Do I live life in reaction, like a target or at my own direction, like an arrow?

Once you assess the emotional aspects of your life, spend some time thinking about how your emotions affect your life. Do you like what you see? Is there anything about your emotional life that does not serve you? Dealing with your emotions is not a straightforward task. It may take some searching. But, a healthy emotional life is essential to achieving balance.

Building a Spiritual Foundation

Building your spiritual foundation is a highly personal undertaking. What inspires you? How do you sustain yourself through the challenges of life today? Your spiritual foundation nourishes you. It is food. Do you find this nourishment in community with others, through organized religion, through your individual spiritual practice, or through another means? Here are some things to look at as you set your spiritual foundation.

> Where do you turn in times of crisis?
> How do you find community?
> What do you need to sustain you?
> How do you celebrate your life?
> What inspires you?

Once you assess the spiritual aspects of your life, see where the holes are. Do you already have a strong spiritual foundation? If you do, congratulations—move on to the development of your mental foundation. If not, spend some quiet time asking yourself what spiritual sustenance you need. Then, begin exploring. Create your spiritual life. Make it strong. Allow it to nourish you and put strong intention into building and sustaining it.

> *"Find your spiritual center—*
> *whatever that means for you—and don't lose it."*
> —Bradley S. Jacobs, chairman and CEO of United Rentals, Inc.
> quoted in *The Way to the Top*, Donald Trump

Building a Mental Foundation

No surprises here, this foundation of balance centers on your mind. It is about honoring your mind but also keeping it in its place. Your mind is an incredible tool in achieving balance. But it can also run away with you and create great imbalance. Setting your mental foundation is about integrating your mind with your physical, emotional, and spiritual life. This is not an easy task. Here are some things to look at as you set your mental foundation.

> Do I value the role my mind plays in my life?
> Do I use my mind to its full capacity and to my advantage?
> Do I ever allow my mind to sabotage me? How?
> How do my mind and my stress levels interrelate?
> What inner voices do I contend with?

Once you assess the role your mind plays in your life, start to develop a relationship with your mind. Observe how it works as you go through a day. Note if it assists you or sabotages you. Look at how you value your mind and how it relates with other aspects of your foundation. Begin to understand the healthy role your mind can play in your life. Put things in place to support that role.

Balance is Dynamic

Balance is dynamic as opposed to static; it is ever changing. Try balancing on one foot. You will notice that perfect balance is a fleeting moment. For the most part, you are constantly making adjustments—sometimes major, sometimes minor—to achieve balance. It is a process of give and take. Balance never looks the same each day. How do you deal with the give and take of balance? Focus and living in the present moment are key elements of balance. As the daily demands of your world confront you, a focus on priorities and a sense of reality regarding what is possible will help you through.

As you create a foundation for balance in your life, maintain a sense of flexibility. This will allow you to keep your focus and carry you through as you deal with unexpected demands on your time. At times, this can be a tightrope walk. Flexibility and focus may seem incompatible to you. But, truly they are not. If you are walking on a tightrope, you keep your focus on your destination while constantly adjusting to the give and take of the rope and your position on it. Balance requires the same.

A key task, upon which rested Donald's choice of the first Apprentice, was when Bill Rancic and his team had to manage a golf tournament at Trump National Golf Club in Westchester, New York. In addition to many details to attend to, a number of surprises came up that easily could have set the team off balance, hindering their chances of winning. When Donald arrived he told the room that he was going to fire Bill "like a dog" if he screws up. Bill kept his cool. The morning of the tournament there was a delay because of overnight frost on the course, which hindered playing conditions. Donald told Bill that he wanted to play by ten-thirty A.M. Then, a sponsor's advertising poster was missing. The team fanned out to find it. Bill found it in a dumpster—a disaster averted! Each of these things could have set the team off balance. Honestly, the team did get frazzled and at times, Bill seemed frantic. But overall, the team responded to the situations, regained their balance and pulled off their task, leading to Bill's selection as The Apprentice.

As you balance your life, your priorities and focus will inevitably change. Remember the Coaches Training Institute balance wheel discussed earlier? The proportions of each section of your wheel will change as you maintain balance. For example, if you move to a new city, the amount of time you spend on your physical environment may increase greatly, as you find a place to live. Or, if there is a major deadline at work, your time on your career may increase. Your life adjusts to its realities. In the midst of it all you maintain balance. If you have built a strong foundation for balance, you can make the adjustments you need to as your life changes. You know what you need to maintain balance.

As you begin to build a strong foundation of balance in your life, here are some things to consider. They are commit to balance, rebalance when necessary, and keep it balanced.

Commit to Balance

The word commitment brings different responses in people. But whatever way you cut it, you must have commitment to yourself to achieve balance. What does the word commitment mean to you? Does the concept energize you? Does it make you shrink? Does it intimidate you? Whatever you feel, commitment is necessary to achieving a balanced life. *Webster's Dictionary* defines commitment as "carrying into action deliberately." That's a good starting point for committing to balance in your life.

Begin with an exploration of what you have already committed to in your life. Are you committed to your family, your work, certain principles, or perhaps a political or charitable cause? Whatever it is, look at how you established your commitment and how you maintain it. Then apply your experience to achieving balance in your life. Here are some ways to commit to balance in your life.

Set Your Goals

Define several goals that, if achieved, will create lasting balance in your life. Set dates by which you will achieve your goals. Find the support you need to stick to it.

Take Action

If the best course for you is to jump right in, take an action immediately that moves you closer to balance. For example, join a gym and commit to going twice weekly. Or, commit to spending no more than a certain number of hours at work each week.

Eliminate What's Not Working

Get started by identifying the aspects of your life that are not in balance. You may not be getting enough sleep or are not eating right. Or you may be putting off getting that physical exam at the doctor's.

Commit to ending habits that do not contribute to balance in your life. Pick one now and change that behavior for good.

Make a Plan

Visualize your life as you want it to be. For each element of your ideal balanced life, set a plan to achieve it. Identify the steps you need to take and begin. Review your progress regularly and take it one step at a time.

Commitment to balance is about putting yourself first. You will not achieve balance unless you prioritize *you*. Some of us are conditioned to equate self-care with selfishness. Your self-care allows you to have what you need to give your best. If you feel guilty as you set out to achieve balance, let that guilt go. It does not serve you. By putting yourself first, you can give your best self to others.

When you commit to balance, you can see the road before you. With commitment comes the clarity and strength you need to change your life. It's up to you. Make a commitment today to achieve balance in your life.

Rebalance When Necessary

We have looked at how to maintain balance when one part of your life is particularly demanding. By making balance a priority, you can make it through these times. But, what happens when your life has been out of balance over a long period of time? How do you rebalance your life and get back on track?

Using the word r-e-b-a-l-a-n-c-e, here are some steps you can take.

Reassess

When you first identify that you have been out of balance, take some time to reassess your life. Look at your present level of balance. What is missing or not working well? What changed to create this situation? What is needed to regain your balance?

Energize

Focus on regaining your balance. Create the energy you need to do what you want to do. Set your intent on physical, emotional, spiritual, and mental levels to regain balance.

Begin

Determine what is needed in your life in order to regain balance. Identify what actions you need to take. Prepare to act.

Arrange

Put in place what you need to act. Organize your life so that you are able to do what is needed to regain balance. Create support structures.

Leave

Let go of aspects of your life that no longer serve you. Let bad habits go. Leave behind anything that gets in the way of your regaining balance.

Act

Make the changes needed to regain balance. Emphasize the doing. Make balance a part of your life again.

Nurture

As time passes and you regain balance, nurture yourself on a regular basis. Regaining balance can create stress and requires strength. Give yourself the support you need to succeed.

Catch

There will be times that you slip and lose your balance momentarily. Be aware and notice when this happens. Catch yourself and do what is needed to get back on track.

Ease

As you regain balance, find the flow. Create a sense of ease with the patterns of balance. Let balance integrate into your life.

Keep It Balanced

Here's where the challenge comes in. How do you maintain a balanced life? It is not an easy task with the demands of your life knocking at your door. Maintaining balance requires keeping your physical, emotional, spiritual, and mental selves finely tuned and able to withstand the ups and downs of life. You have created your foundation, now begin to build on it and keep it strong.

Physical balance depends on your ability to maintain good health, support yourself through your work, and create a physical environment that supports you. Emotional balance depends on meeting your emotional needs, expressing your creativity, and handling change in your life. Spiritual balance depends on giving yourself the spiritual sustenance you need, creating community, and living your life in accordance with your values. Mental balance depends on understanding the role your mind plays in your life, not letting your mind control you or get out of control, and integrating your mind with your physical, emotional, and spiritual selves.

At different times, you will put more emphasis on one part of your life over another. Remember that balance is dynamic as opposed to static. Balance is not about staying in one state all the time. Balance is the ability to stay in relative proportion to a state of harmony, as your life changes.

RECAP

Acknowledge all parts of yourself. In a wheel, all spokes are aligned and in motion.

The ability to choose. Discrimination is the essence of balance.

A strong foundation. Take care of yourself physically, emotionally, spiritually, and mentally.

Balance is dynamic. Perfect balance is a fleeting moment. You are constantly making adjustments.

EXERCISES

1. Designate a toleration-free day. Let your family, friends, and others know what you are doing. Tell them you are going to spend the day honoring yourself. When something comes up that you do not want to tolerate—don't tolerate it. Be civil, but spend the day in a life-affirming way. At the end of the day, identify the tolerations that you eluded and make note of them. Give some thought to what occurs in your life when it is out of balance.

2. Create a list of warning signs that signal when you are losing balance. For each sign, create a "911" plan detailing what you will do to restore balance when that sign appears.

3. Create time to look at the foundation you have created for your life. List the elements of your physical, emotional, spiritual, and mental foundations. What parts of your foundation are secure? Where do you need reinforcement?

CHAPTER SIX
LESSON FIVE: HAVE A STRATEGY

"I am a good person who knows how to fight for what she believes in." —Omarosa Manigault-Stallworth

Omarosa Manigault-Stallworth was a lightning rod in the first season of *The Apprentice*. She infuriated some and alienated others. But, one thing you can say about her is she did it her way. I think it is safe to say Omarosa had a strategy. What were the components of her strategy? Here are a few of my thoughts after observing her on the show.

If I had to guess at Omarosa's strategy, the main components may have been: stand out, make my presence known, exhibit extreme confidence at all times, do what I can to set others off balance when it will be to my advantage, do not let others get the better of me—ever, and always act in my own interest.

From the start, Omarosa stood out. She is a beautiful woman, with a striking appearance. As for exhibiting confidence, I never heard her admit she made a mistake. She frequently blamed others for problems or if her team failed. It was never her fault.

Omarosa is skilled at setting others off balance. Early in the show she was already fighting with Katrina. In the third week, Jesse, the project manager for that week gave Omarosa and Katrina separate tasks to keep them away from each other. In week five, Kristi thought

Omarosa was setting her team up to lose when she found out that money was missing. Omarosa frequently provoked her teammates. By their reactions, it was clear she was succeeding. They were allowing her to get under their skin. One time Donald commented in the boardroom on Omarosa's lack of social skills, but was that part of her strategy?

I never saw Omarosa let her teammates know they were getting the better of her. I do not know what she was feeling inside, but her outward demeanor exhibited confidence at all times. There was one exception, when she was in the boardroom and thought she was at risk she lost her composure in front of the group. But in the main, she kept her cool.

I do not think Omarosa ever stopped acting in her own interest. When the contest was down to Kwame and Bill, Omarosa came back and was on Kwame's team. She did not exhibit much interest in helping Kwame win. It hurt her team when she would not reveal what happened in a phone call with casino staff. My guess: if she revealed what happened it would not be in her best interest.

Omarosa's strategy, in the end, was not a winning one. She was not selected as The Apprentice. She did not have the respect of her teammates. She was not an audience favorite. But, she did have a strategy and kept to it. She was high profile. She got through a good amount of the contest. Viewers talked about her, and she got a lot of press after the show. Perhaps her strategy did work for her. It depends on what she wanted to accomplish. Only Omarosa knows.

As a leader, having a strategy gives you a significant advantage. You can have strategies for a variety of your endeavors, big and small. Your strategy sets a path for you. It helps you organize yourself and others to get things done. It gives you a benchmark on which to evaluate your progress, and it focuses your energies. A strategy allows you to structure your thinking and activities. As you approach a project, your strategy addresses what needs to happen and how you will achieve it. It sets out incremental steps and timelines. It serves as a guide for you and other team members.

Having a strategy gives you direction. You have a focus. You know your ultimate goal. You know how you want to get there as steps are laid out for you. Your timing is set. In your analysis, you have anticipated obstacles that you may face. Conversely, if you do not have a strategy, you can be at a disadvantage. If you are competing, your competition may have a strategy and hold the advantage. You could start out on one track and find midstream that it's the wrong one. Your team's efforts can become unfocused.

Strategies are both for you as a leader and for your projects. Strategic thinking has many uses. Develop a mindset that having a strategy will help you. Sharpen your abilities to think strategically and develop strategic plans. Here are some concepts that are central to your strategic thinking as you develop your leadership capabilities.

Design Your Life

My first life coach was Leslie Lupinsky. Her company is called Design Your Life. Leslie was my coach as I created and developed my own coaching practice, and she helped me through a huge transition. I owe her a lot for her excellent guidance and coaching through a challenging time. The name of her company has stayed with me.

You can design your life. Have a plan for where you want your life and career to go. Why design your life? It is about creating your destiny. It may seem a contradiction in terms to create your destiny. There is a destiny for you, a path laid out in front of you. But, you must walk the path to know it. Your walking is fueled by your intent. It is a delicate balance: be open to the clues you are given as to your destiny, but also set your intent to be in movement on your path. My transition to coaching involved this delicate balance. In 1995, I owned an environmental consulting firm. My business partner told me she was thinking of retiring early and leaving the business.

That opened up a set of questions for me. Did I want to continue the business on my own? What did I want to do in the next phase of my career? Did I want to stay in the environmental field? I opened myself to the possibility of change and waited to see what showed up.

Initially, I was considering my options in the environmental field. But, nothing seemed right. Then I began to explore starting a nonprofit organization to help women in business. I asked a group of outstanding women I knew to work with me in this endeavor. My work with them set my focus and attention on what women needed to succeed in business. We designed a structure to address what we perceived were the real needs women have in business.

In the summer of 1996, while at a seminar, I met a woman who was training to be a coach. I asked her what coaching was, and found the concept interested me. I realized that our approach to the nonprofit organization was based on many of the same principles as the coaching profession. In August of that same summer, I took my first class at the Coaches Training Institute. I loved it and soon was on my way to becoming a coach. In this experience, I had designed my life through my intent and allowing my destiny to unfold. Clearly, coaching was part of my destiny. But my intent was critical, too. I had to begin exploring options to get to a place where I was receptive to coaching. By being open to the clues before me regarding my destiny and setting my intent to move forward, I found my next step.

Designing your life is an important element in having a strategy. Here are some things to consider as you design your life. They are: it is your life, you have the power to create it, things may not always be as they seem, and you are the architect.

It is Your Life

This may seem a simple concept, but it amazes me how often we can give control of our life to other people or circumstances. Often, giving away control happens subtly; it is not always a conscious act. But it happens, nonetheless. As you design your life, remember that you are in the driver's seat.

What does this mean that you are in the driver's seat? The candidates on *The Apprentice* could say their success or failure was not in their hands. They might reason that the decision was Donald Trump's to make, they could not control the tasks they are given, or that the show was a much bigger force than their individual participation. But, if they think this way, my guess is they can't win. Each candidate must place him or herself in the driver's seat. How can a candidate do this? By holding themselves accountable for their performance. By using their brain to understand and master the environment they are operating in. By fine-tuning their best performance in each task. Each candidate gives themselves the best chance of winning by placing him or herself in the driver's seat.

How can you give away control of your life? By feeling that there are people and circumstances that control you. You always have control of your own responses and actions in any situation. You may not control a situation or a person, but you control your life in the face of whatever happens to you. You can give away control of your life by allowing yourself to become overwhelmed or by feeling trapped in a situation. These feelings leave you powerless. How can you live your life in the driver's seat? By seeing yourself at the steering wheel. You are not a victim. You control the direction of your life. You may not control what comes up on the road, but you do steer the car.

You Have the Power to Design It

Power is a word that elicits varying reactions. Some people love power. Others find it vile. People define power in various ways. Power as I am using it here is your knowledge that you have what you need to design your life. What do you need to design your life? You need commitment, insight, good judgment, and strength. Commitment is about sticking with it: acknowledging your part in creating your life and accepting that responsibility. Insight is needed in order to read or analyze the events in your life correctly. Good judgment involves acting in your best interest and in integrity. Strength is needed when you accept that the buck stops with you. You also need strength to weather the tests and challenges you experience. It takes strength to believe in yourself, as well.

If you feel powerless, it behooves you to start working on developing your sense of power. How can you do this? Start by identifying all the areas of your life in which you feel you have control. Affirm your power in all these areas. You may say I have power in the quality of my work. Or, I have power over where and for whom I work—it is my choice.

Second, identify any areas of your life where you feel you do not have control. Look carefully at them. What is the source of your feeling of a lack of control? If it is a person, why does that person hold control? Is there something you can do to take control back? If it is a circumstance, what can you do to respond to it? If you analyze each situation where you feel a lack of control, you will begin to see ways that you can get back in the driver's seat.

Too many times we give away our power. Consciously or subconsciously we convince ourselves we are powerless and we act that way. On the first season of *The Apprentice* it is possible that Kwame gave away his power by thinking he could not fire Omarosa. He thought he had to keep her on his team and give her a role in his final project—the one that would determine whether he won or lost. A lot was at stake. Omarosa's acts hurt his chances of winning. When Kwame came into the boardroom with Donald, Donald asked Kwame why he hadn't fired Omarosa. Donald said he would have. Kwame replied that he didn't know he had the option to fire her and he needed all three people to complete his task. Where did Kwame give away his power? He thought Donald would not allow him to fire Omarosa and he thought that he needed three people on his team, even though Omarosa was hurting his effort and draining energy from the team.

> **Let Go of Your Illusions**
>
> Select a person you work with. What would you say is their agenda at work? How does this change the way you see them?

Things May Not Always Be as They Seem

To design your life you have to give away illusions and develop the ability to see things as they really are. In work situations, things may not always be as they seem. To design your life, you must be able to see the field you are playing on. Otherwise, you are playing a game that does not fit with the game you are really in.

What do I mean by this? Here are some examples of truths that you may not see at first glance.

People have agendas. Although, on the surface, the intent appears to be to work together to get a job done, that may not be the primary objective of the people you work with. Some people may be there to further their own agenda first. Others may need to control certain situations to go their own way rather than in the interest of getting the job done.

Not everything is communicated openly in the workplace. Hidden agendas may exist. I remember doing a management assessment for a client. I approached the job thinking that the client had asked for the assessment because they wanted to improve their operations. I set about the task doing the best analysis I could and making solid recommendations for improvement. After the job was over, I realized that there had been a hidden agenda in the request. My client wanted to see if my assessment would reveal inadequacies in the performance of one of his rivals. My assessment was a tool not for improvement, but for political gain.

Not everyone has your best interests at heart. Here's an illusion to toss quickly. Do you think that, ultimately, *The Apprentice* candidates have their team members' best interests at heart? To the extent that they want their team to win, they do. But each candidate knows that the prize will go to only one of them. If they can further their individual interest over that of the team's, they will.

You Are the Architect

Designing your life comes down to knowing that you are the architect of your strategy. You create your life. No one has absolute power over you, no matter what the situation. You have power, unless you choose to give it away. As the architect of

Hidden Agendas

Look back over your career. Find an instance where there was a hidden agenda that it took you some time to see.

your own strategy, take responsibility. Using this metaphor, as the architect, find your site. Make sure it suits you. Design the structure for your life. Engineer its creation. Handle the problems and challenges that come your way while you are building. Bring in the resources you need along the way. Set your standards high. Build a skyscraper. Go for the best and believe you can have it.

Focus

Focus is essential to creating and implementing your strategy. Without focus, nothing happens. When Donald Trump gives *The Apprentice* candidates a task, one of the very first things they must do is focus. What do they need to do to get the task done and win? Who are their teammates for this project? What are each teammate's strengths and weaknesses related to the task? How will they organize?

In today's world, there are numerous demands on your time and attention. In many ways, it is not possible to keep up with all of it. If you want to succeed in your strategy, focus is essential. Start by identifying the top priorities in your strategy. Then, spend your time honoring those priorities and getting them done. Once you have identified what you must do, commit to maintaining your focus to achieve it.

By focusing on your priorities, you bring your time, energy, and attention to the task at hand. With focus, distractions begin to fall away and you create a clear path to accomplishment. How can you begin to develop the focus you need to accomplish your goals? Start by letting go of the distractions in your life. Follow that by letting go of things that no longer serve you. Decide on your priorities and honor them. Then, work to maintain your focus.

Focus is not always an easy pursuit. It will take your strong dedication and commitment. But, if you maintain your focus, you will begin to see rewards. Things will get done and you will see movement towards your goals. The quality of your work will improve. Your stress level will eventually decrease, because you will know how you want to spend your time.

Here are some of the elements in creating your focus. They are:

setting your priorities, meaningful movement, maintaining focus, and dealing with what comes up.

Setting Your Priorities

With the many demands on your time, how do you set your priorities? First, set your work priorities within the context of a balanced life, as discussed in Chapter Five. Without balance, your efforts to focus can crash and burn. Decide how much time is available to you to meet your goals. Set your priorities accordingly. If you have twenty priorities that, in reality, will take five years to achieve, you are setting yourself up for frustration. Be reasonable about what you can do.

Second, identify your goals and the steps you need to take to achieve them. Be thorough in this task. This is your road map. If you miss a significant step, you may encounter setbacks or delays. Get input from others whom you trust and who can advise you.

Third, prioritize and organize the steps you have identified. Do the steps need to be done in a certain order? Do some steps depend on the outcome or completion of other steps? What are the steps most critical to your succeeding and reaching your goal? Once you have taken these steps, identify your priorities.

As I began my coaching career, so many new possibilities opened up for me. My creativity was soaring and I was jazzed. Every effort seemed worthwhile. But I soon realized that I was not getting where I wanted to in building my practice. I was fragmenting my time. I was over-optimistic about how many things I could accomplish. My focus was scattered. I was not completing things. Several years ago I developed a daily system that continues to work for me. At the start of each day, I set three to five priorities, and I set them in the context of the time I have available for my business that day. For example, I may have a meeting outside my office or a yoga class. Once I set the priorities, I commit that I will not do other tasks until those priorities are completed. For me, it works; I keep my focus on priorities. At the end of the day, I feel a sense of accomplishment and am motivated to continue towards accomplishing my goals.

Meaningful Movement

A critical element in reaching your goals is meaningful movement. Focus takes on a different nuance here. You may have identified your goals and the steps to achieve them. As you progress, it behooves you to ask yourself if what you are doing is the best way to get you where you want to go. Meaningful movement is taking actions that get you to your goal in the most efficient and effective manner.

In one task on *The Apprentice*, Donald asked the teams to sell his new product, Trump Ice. It is bottled drinking water and teams were tasked to distribute the most water in order to win. As the teams approached restaurants to sell Trump Ice, they found that they did not have sufficient storage space for large orders. This limited how much the teams could sell and was a source of frustration. Toward the end of their time for the task, Troy came up with a brilliant strategy that illustrates what meaningful movement is. He suggested that the team sell several weeks worth of water to be delivered in increments. The strategy became a winner for the team. Instead of allowing storage capacities to limit them, they spent the same amount of time selling long-term contracts.

Another aspect of meaningful movement is to make sure you are spending your time well. Develop a time frame for completing each step. Estimate the time needed to complete a task, considering the time you have available to do it. Measure yourself against the timeline. Are you meeting your deadline? Are you working efficiently? Are you on track to meeting your goal? Monitor your progress against the timeline.

As you assess whether you are in meaningful movement, you can review and revise your strategy. You will maximize your efficiency in reaching your goals.

"The man with the plan leads the way."
—Paul R. Gudonis, chairman and CEO of Genuity, Inc.
quoted in *The Way to the Top*, Donald Trump

Maintaining Focus

Once you succeed in creating focus, you meet another challenge: maintaining focus. How do you keep your focus over time while encountering distractions, crises, and new demands on your time? It is a daily effort. Here are some ways to support yourself so that you can maintain focus.

Begin each day with quiet time. During this time (it can be as short as five minutes), look at the day ahead and what you want to accomplish. Identify your priorities for the day and decide what you will do to get them done.

Eliminate unnecessary distractions. Keep your focus on the "must do's." Do not make that unnecessary phone call or do a task that is not critical to accomplishing your priorities for that day.

Allow for disruptions. Inevitably, things will occur during a day to pull you off focus. These are things that *must* be done, for example, a crisis that must be handled at work or an unexpected development that demands your attention. Give your full attention to what needs to get done and then return to your focus. By allowing for unavoidable disruptions, you keep yourself centered and can return to your previous focus when the disruption is handled. Disruptions, when not handled properly, can pull you off center, take much more time to handle than necessary, and can leave you frazzled and upset. The unexpected will happen, you can count on that.

Write it down. Writing down things you want to focus on can be very helpful. You can do this on multiple levels. Start by identifying the things you want to focus on in the big picture. Establish your focus for the year. Then daily, write down what you will accomplish that day related to your focus for the year. Have the daily list visible, so that if distractions occur, you can look at the list and maintain your focus.

Develop your own structure for maintaining focus and stick to it. It is only by maintaining your focus that you will get where you want to be.

Dealing With What Comes Up

Effective focus depends on your ability to avoid distraction. Let's look a bit more deeply at how you can deal with things that can pull you off your focus. What are the kinds of things that can come up? Some of them can be internally driven. You could be experiencing fear about where your actions will bring you. You may or may not recognize the fear but it is there. So, you find things to distract yourself from continuing. You may just be plain tired. You do not have energy to continue at the pace you are going. Other things can be externally driven. Your business is experiencing a spurt of growth. Your company is downsizing and you are asked to take on more tasks.

What can you do when things come up that pull you off your focus? First, pull yourself to center so that you can realistically assess the situation and what your options are. Second, look at the current level of balance in your life. Is lack of balance contributing to the situation? Third, develop a plan of action to regain your focus. You may have to delay some steps, but make sure you have a strategy to get back on track.

"If you fail to plan, you are planning to fail."
—Robert J. Laikin, chairman and CEO of Brightpoint, Inc.
quoted in *The Way to the Top*, Donald Trump

Sometimes you have to give in to internal or external influences. When you think this is the case, make sure there are compelling reasons to do so. Then accept the situation. Revise your strategy to accommodate the situation. Other times you don't have to give in. In these cases, your priorities become a factor again. If a circumstance is demanding you do something else, you may face difficult choices. To stick with your focus and priorities, do you have to take strong action? Do you have to take a period of time to change the situation so you can return to your focus?

Sometimes you may find yourself in a circumstance where you have to quit or give up your goal. Avoid this as best you can. When you must, let go with grace, and make the best of the situation. Set a new direction that serves your interest and get in motion again.

Know What it Will Take

As *The Apprentice* candidates face a task, they must be realistic. In most cases, they have just a day or two to complete their task. If they do not make an accurate assessment of what it will take to win, their strategy is worthless. This chapter is about the importance of having a strategy. To have an effective strategy, you must know what it will take to reach your goal.

What does "knowing what it takes" involve? It involves taking both a micro and macro view of the task ahead and identifying what you need to do to get it done. Knowing what it will take demands skill and experience. You have to know yourself or find someone who knows what needs to be done.

Many times, people embark on a task without taking time to identify what they need. They stumble along, taking more time and effort than is necessary. By knowing what it takes when you start out, you increase your chances of success. Here are some factors involved in knowing what it takes. They are: what do you need, getting personal, working with a team, and realigning along the way.

What Do You Need?

When *The Apprentice* candidates received a dossier from Donald that asked them to renovate, refurbish, and furnish an apartment to increase its value, the teams had to determine quickly what they needed. First they needed an apartment, which they would negotiate for with their opposing team. Then they needed a plan for renovating, refurbishing, and furnishing their apartment—quickly. They needed materials, people to do the work, and a tenant. And all of this within a four-thousand-dollar budget! They needed to divide tasks among the team and to learn what they had to do to make their team a winner.

As you begin a project, take some time to know what you need to succeed. Here are some questions to consider.

What skills do you need to complete the project?
Do you have the necessary skills or do you have to bring on other people?
What physical resources do you need?
Where can you get them?
What financial resources do you need?
Where can you get them?
What type of team (if any) do you have to put together?
Where will you find them?
Whose buy-in do you need to be able to proceed?
What challenges or obstacles do you anticipate?
How will you handle them?
What amount of time do you need to complete the project?

Starting with these questions will help you know what it takes as you begin.

Getting Personal

In knowing what it takes, you have to bring it down to the personal as well. In college, a professor of mine told me that if I wanted to be an effective leader, I had to have a wellspring to draw from within. For me, that meant I needed to have inner resources to sustain me. As you begin a project, assess what is needed from you personally. Here are some questions to ask yourself.

What will be required of me physically to complete the project?
What skills will I be using?
What support will I need?
How will this project affect my work/life balance?
What preparation do I need to do?
Do I foresee any interpersonal conflicts involved in this project?
What amount of time is required daily, weekly, and monthly to complete the project?

Once you have considered these questions, put in place whatever you need to take care of yourself personally during the project. This may include provision for time away from the project to rejuvenate, increased physical exercise to deal with expected stress, better eating habits to keep your energy up, people you can call on for advice, time to prepare what is needed, or another support structure to sustain you during the project.

An effective strategy depends on knowing what it will take to complete a project successfully. Your time is well spent in this endeavor.

Working with a Team

As you begin a project you may find yourself working with a team. The project may start out with a team already formed or you may have to form one. Working with a team increases the complexity of a project. You are dealing with group dynamics, a varied skill base, and a need for efficient coordination. You must know what it takes for your team to get the job done. Here are some things to consider.

Address strengths and weaknesses

What are the strengths of your team? Does your strategy capitalize on those strengths? What are the weaknesses of your team? How will you compensate for them?

Communication. How will your team communicate? How will you communicate your strategy to them?

Resources. What resources will your team need? Who is responsible for providing them?

Problem-Solving. What process will you put in place for problem solving? How will you make sure that issues or problems are raised to you or the appropriate team member in a timely manner?

Meeting Their Needs. What are the team's needs? How will you meet them?

If you work with a team, they are essential factors in your success. Know what it will take to get the team working smoothly towards your goal.

> *"How do you lose a rock star?"*
> —Omarosa Manigault-Stallworth

Realign Along the Way

When Donald Trump was building Trump Place on the west side of Manhattan, his plans originally called for tall buildings in his trademark grand style. Early in the project he encountered community opposition to losing the low profile of the area. Donald then redesigned the complex to a series of lower buildings, still retaining the Trump style.

Knowing what it takes involves consistent retuning and realignment of your project to assure you are on the best track toward your goals. To accomplish this, you, as leader, need to build regular checks into your strategy. There are many ways to do this. You can have weekly meetings with staff to review progress and discuss current or potential issues. You can develop interim measures to track your progress. You can develop a process to assure that problems are raised and resolved as early as possible.

As problems arise, you must be ready and nimble to address them. This requires good communication with your team, keeping your own stress level down so that you respond well, knowing your subject so that you can find good solutions, and good radar to identify potential problems or obstacles. It behooves you to assume that things will go wrong. It is the rare project that has no surprises or challenges along the way.

It is about balance. This time it is at the project level. Keep balance between your existing strategy and reality as you go along, and be ready to address problems that come up. Keep your focus on your team's needs. Watch your measures. Stay at the helm and guide. Rebalance and realign as you need to.

As you begin a project, build ways to realign into your strategy. Spell them out. Keep communication strong with and among your team. Identify interim measures, and have contingency plans, in case something goes awry. Build sufficient time into your strategy to address surprises. Determine how you and your team will address problems that arise; realignment keeps you and your project on a steady course to success.

One Step at a Time

When you get down to basics, having a strategy means charting your path one step at a time. You need to be thorough, set your speed, and chart a course. You cannot reach your goal without putting one foot in front of the other, so to speak. Often, people want to reach the top in one great leap. Most of the time, it does not work that way. It takes planning and persistence to reach your goals. The small steps add up. They will get you there. Let's discuss some of the stages involved in taking one step at a time. They are: getting ready, taking the first step, keeping going, and reaching the goal.

Getting Ready

As you begin a project, expend some effort getting ready. Preparation will be a big factor in your eventual success.

What does preparation entail? First, it requires your focus. Look at what is before you.

What do you intend to accomplish?

How will you do it? What do you need in way of resources?

Sometimes it is helpful to write things down. You can create a mission statement for the project. List the resources you will need and where you will get them. List what you need in place before you begin along with the steps involved in the project. You can also create a timeline detailing what will be done and when.

Get yourself ready, too.

What do you need to begin the project?

Do you have the time available that this project will require?

Do you have the financial resources you need?

Do you need to make any changes in how things are now before you begin?

Do you need to brush up on a new subject or develop a skill in order to be ready?

Be sure to get yourself in good shape physically, emotionally, spiritually, and mentally to begin.

Next, get everything in place before you begin. Take the time to organize your life and the project so that your start is smooth. Then, honor your beginning. Find a way to mark that you are embarking on something new. A marker may be a celebration, buying something new for the project, an announcement to colleagues or family, or simply self-acknowledgment that you are beginning.

Finally, get yourself psyched for what lies ahead. Get excited. Believe that you can do it. Imagine yourself at the finish and the good things the project will bring.

Taking the First Step

Lynn Andrews once said to me that the muses come when there is movement. We were talking about my writing and she was encouraging me to write every day. In my own life and my work with clients, I often focus on taking the first step. Sometimes it is not an easy step to take—we can build up fears about the first step. By getting ourselves in motion, we are affirming that we are doing something. We are acknowledging that we are proceeding.

When I look back on my life I am amazed at the diversions I have created to keep myself from taking the first step! My reluctance, I think, was subconscious. The diversions had a higher purpose: to keep me from taking the first step. For in movement, was acceptance that I would proceed and set a goal to accomplish something. In movement also, was the possibility that I would fail or that my life would change in some way.

In humans, there is a natural inclination toward the status quo.

We do not always relish stepping out of our comfort zone. These attitudes can make it very difficult to take the first step in a new endeavor. If you find yourself reluctant to take a first step for a project, take some time to look at what is going on. Are you fearful about some aspect of the project? Are you unsure whether you can do it? Is there something you are doubtful about? Will the project bring change to your life or bring you out of your comfort zone? Do you feel prepared to begin? Once you get a sense regarding what is going on, set your determination to take your first step soon.

If you are reluctant, find the way that is best for you to begin. Different projects may require different approaches. Perhaps making sure you are fully prepared will help you. If so, do what you need to do. Perhaps accepting that you are out of your comfort zone will help. In this acceptance, you can create a support structure for yourself. It may be friends, mentors, or practices that will support you. Perhaps dealing with your attitudes about change will help. This is something you can do over time. Get familiar with the fears change creates for you. Tackle them one-by-one. Accept that change is an undeniable part of life. Find the good things change can bring into your life. Sometimes, there is no choice but to get in movement, to blast through it and take the first step. Whatever you do, avoid dancing in circles around that first step. There is nothing to gain. Your first step gets you going. Often, it's all downhill from there.

Keeping Going

You've taken the first step. Now your focus can shift to keeping going. Keeping going can involve a number of things. Persistence, endurance, skill, belief in yourself, and positive thinking can all be involved. With the proper planning, you already have set the course for your project. Now, it is up to you to follow the course and deal with what comes up.

As you progress on a project, what things can come up and how can you deal with them? Perhaps you come up against an unanticipated delay. Analyze the impact the delay will have on your project.

Try to find ways to avoid the delay, such as bringing on additional resources or eliminating an underlying cause of the delay. If you cannot avoid it, make the necessary adjustments in your strategy and inform the appropriate people. Perhaps you lose resources on the project. Analyze whether you can do the project without them. Do your best to replace them, and make adjustments in your strategy.

Sometimes keeping going involves just you. Perhaps you have lost motivation or you feel discouraged. Perhaps things have gotten out of balance. If this is the case, bring yourself to the present moment and see where you are. What do you have to do to get yourself going again? Give yourself time and space to do it. Sometimes what happens can create a situation where you cannot go on with the project. First, do everything possible to continue. But, if the best choice is to end the project, bring yourself to a place of acceptance. Do what you need to do to close the project well. Take some time to identify the lessons learned.

Persistence is often is the key to success. You may be a tortoise or a hare, but keeping going is what matters. Develop your skills to carry through. They will serve you well.

Reaching the Goal

As you approach the end of your project, take a moment to assess where you are. Check your progress against your plan.

Are you on track?
Will all your goals be reached?
Have you used your measures?
What is now between you and the finish line?
Are any adjustments needed or can you proceed as planned?

Once you complete this assessment, get back in movement and finish.

As you finish a project acknowledge what you have done. Acknowledgment is an important value in the coaching profession.

Coaches always encourage their clients to acknowledge their successes and even their failures. This acknowledgment allows you to learn. It allows you to take in what you have done. So often we rush right to the next thing that has to be done without proper acknowledgment of what has just occurred. Acknowledgment also allows for proper endings. Evaluate how the project went, what you learned, what you might have done differently, and what worked. Then, move on to your next project, wiser from what you have just learned.

RECAP
Design your Life. Create a fulfilling life.
Focus. You must have strong intent.
Know what it will take. Understand the environment you are in.
One step at a time. The importance of planning and persistence.

EXERCISES
1. Practice developing a strategy. For next week, set a plan for what you want to accomplish and how you will do it. Set measures for mid-week to assess your progress. At the end of the week, review how your strategy worked.

2. Set three priorities to accomplish in a day. Stick to them. What have you learned by doing this?

3. Identify one recent accomplishment you had, then find a way to acknowledge it.

CHAPTER SEVEN
LESSON SIX: THINK OUTSIDE THE BOX

"Protégé did not think outside the box and took a severe thumping." —Donald Trump

As the Protégé and Versacorp teams set out to manage one shift of a pedicab company in New York City, they both wanted to win. They had to come up with a strategy. In this task, more than any other, we saw the importance of thinking outside the box. As the Protégé team managed their shift, they lifted their heads and encountered a shock. Their strategy centered on driver incentives and pre-paid ride cards. As a Versacorp pedicab rode by, they saw an advertisement on the back of the pedicab. Versacorp had sold ads on the pedicabs. The Protégé team realized at that moment that they were in trouble. Versacorp's winning strategy resulted from thinking outside the box.

A leader must be able to go beyond convention and think creatively. Everyone is creative. It is more about uncovering your innate creativity than learning to be creative. How often do you place value on being able to think creatively at work? We get so caught up in the culture of our workplaces, in doing things "right," in interacting with others, and in succeeding, we have no space to think creatively. Creativity needs space. You need time to be on your own and nurture your creativity. You need a quiet mind to access your creativity. You need to give yourself permission to be creative and not worry about what others think. You need to let your mind go where it has never gone before.

Many times workplaces stifle creativity. One of my favorite business books is David Whyte's *The Heart Aroused: Poetry and the Preservation of the Soul in Corporate America*. David Whyte is a poet who has a successful corporate consulting practice. The book speaks of how work both emboldens and strangles us in the very same minute and how much the wellsprings of our creativity are stopped at the source by the pressures of an organization.

Think of your workplace. If you work alone, think of your working environment and the market you work in. What are the elements of your workplace that encourage creativity? What elements stifle creativity? You may say your goal at work is to succeed and you are going to play the game the way it is. But, if you want to lead, you need vision and creativity. These attributes come from within. You must nurture them so they will appear. True leaders have accessed their creativity and use it.

Creativity is about your internal voice or soul. Your voice is unique. For some, creativity is artistic ability. For others, it is about vision in business or politics. There are as many types of creativity as there are people in the world. Accessing your creativity is a journey. You take it alone, although there are muses and mentors along the way. Accessing your creativity rewards you in many areas. Your creativity can open a path to your passion in life and allows you to express who you really are. Your creativity brings you satisfaction and draws others to you. Your creativity can bring success as your workplace confronts non-ordinary challenges. Creativity brings innovation, a well-recognized asset in the marketplace.

As you access your creativity, there is no room for judgment or self-criticism. There are no outside standards that are relevant to your journey of creativity. My journey to creativity was greatly influenced by my work with Lynn Andrews. At Lynn's annual gatherings, participants create a piece of art. It may be a mask, a shield or basket. Lynn asks that our art be a self expression. It is not about following the rules of fine art. When I started at these gatherings, I was very intimidated that I had to create. Lynn always reassured us it was about self-expression, not mastery, and I gradually let go of my fears. I saw beauty in my creations because I had put part of myself into them. I accepted that I was creative and that my creativity was the expression of my inner voice.

Do you want to take the journey to access your own creativity? Here are some concepts to get you on your way.

Forget Safe

Do you think the Versacorp team was thinking safety when they came up with the idea to put ads on the pedicabs? I don't think so. There were many risks in their strategy. Would anyone buy the ads? To my knowledge, there were not any ads currently sold by the pedicab company. During the task one of the ads fell off a pedicab. But, in the end Versacorp won with a wide margin and was rewarded for thinking outside the box. Donald Trump would not be where he is today if safety was his primary value. There's nothing wrong with some safety. A leader however, does not let a need for safety limit his or her vision or creativity.

I live in the high Mojave Desert of southern California, in the Antelope Valley. Our area is known for its flight testing programs and facilities and is ripe with flight test legends and pilots. It is fascinating for me to hear how flight test programs push the edge of the envelope. What is that drive to go to the edge? I think the people in these programs have let free their creativity and vision. They see possibilities where others do not. They must unleash their creativity to solve the problems and challenges they encounter. They are true leaders.

Here are some things to think about. They are: leaders lead, cushion a fall, take the journey, and muster the courage.

Leaders Lead

First, you must consciously decide if you want to be a leader. There is both good and bad involved in leading. Being a leader can put you in a solitary place. You begin to stand out from others. Your decisions are on your shoulders and you either enjoy or suffer through the outcome. You are drawing on your own abilities and cannot always rely on others. Do you want to lead? If the answer is yes, commit yourself to it and hold on for the ride!

Most leaders have spent time developing their leadership skills. They may learn in a trial by fire situation or they may learn over time. What are the qualities you want to embody as a leader? Take some time to think about them. Leaders often are intelligent. You have innate smarts, but you can also develop more. You can read about your professional field, you can develop your skills on the job, through schooling, or through a mentor. You can keep your mind active and challenged. True leaders have compassion—an understanding of the feelings of others. I say true leaders because there are leaders who do not have compassion. They disregard others to serve only their interests. They can lead, but they usually do not inspire the loyalty or admiration of others. You can develop compassion by putting people first in situations. Develop your awareness of what others feel and want. Communicate with people. Be aware of your own wants and feelings. Look at the human side of situations.

Business leaders have business savvy. They understand the game they are in and how to play it well. They are always students of their game. They keep up with the competition and new developments. They know how to move situations to their own advantage. You can develop business savvy by immersing yourself in the game. Watch the good players, know your business well, and keep yourself on the cutting edge. Do not shy away from challenging situations. Take them on and learn from your successes and failures. Leaders know how to accurately judge people and situations.

Donald Trump has to know this. As a negotiator, he must read people quickly and accurately to win. He must deal with government regulators. He must know what his customers will buy. The best way to develop accurate judgment is to put yourself in situations that require it. Become a student of human nature. Observe all interactions you are in for clues to how people behave. You can read up on negotiating skills. You can read books on human nature or biographies of leaders. You can get in good touch with your own feelings as you negotiate or have to make decisions.

As you face a decision or negotiation, think it out ahead of time. Who are the players? What are their agendas? What do they stand to win or lose? What do you want? Then, once the decision is made or negotiation complete, look back on your initial analysis and how accurate it was.

At some point in your life, you will have to jump into leadership. Take action and lead. Look for opportunities to lead at work. If you do not find them at work, find them elsewhere. You can join a professional or business or charitable organization. Work your way up to a leadership position. Volunteer for leadership opportunities whenever you can, both inside and outside work.

As you lead, what are you finding? Do you want to lead? What are your strengths and weaknesses as a leader? How do you want to further develop your leadership abilities. You are on your way.

Cushion a Fall

"Forget safe" does not mean to be foolhardy. There are many opportunities to fall and fail. You don't have to run headlong into all of them. Pick your risks carefully. Create ways to cushion your fall. If you are going to fall, make sure you've done everything you can to succeed.

First, know your stuff. If you are undertaking a task, prepare in the best way possible. Know your field. Know the strengths and limitations in your strategy. Know what can go wrong and what you have available to you if it does.

Second accept that there is risk in every endeavor. Consider whether the risk involved is acceptable risk. Can you weather things going wrong or failing? What do you have to lose? What will you do to get back on your feet again?

Third, think before you leap. Know the pros and cons of going forward. Do what you can to minimize the cons.

Fourth, if you do fall, brush yourself off. Learn the lessons of the situation and begin again.

Donald Trump has had some ups and downs in his career. He seems always to bounce back and be on the top again. I'm sure he knows how to cushion a fall. He also has confidence. Confidence in your abilities is a huge asset in cushioning a fall. This confidence comes both from within and from experience. You must believe in yourself. Take some time with this.

> What is your profession?
> What are your qualifications for doing this work?
> What are your skills? What are your innate abilities?
> What have you succeeded in? How have you recovered from your failures?
> What do you have to draw on from within?
> What support system is available for you?

As you answer these questions, don't you think you can say confidently that you believe in yourself and your ability to succeed?

Revise your attitudes about failure. Mistakes and failures are part of life. Can you think of anyone who has not made a mistake or failed in some way? If you do make a mistake or fail, accept responsibility for it. Do what you have to do to correct it. Make a point to learn from any mistake or failure.

> What went wrong?
> What could you have done differently?
> What outside factors contributed?
> Could you have done anything about them?

Bring the lessons into your future endeavors. There is no point in repeating mistakes or failures.

There is also no point in being negative about mistakes or failures. Negativity is a downward spiral. You can get lost in it. It can seriously drain your energy. It can color the way you see the world and any future opportunity. Guard against negativity in your life and work. Instead, see opportunities in mistakes and failures. You may need some time to get yourself back on track, but do it as soon as you can. Sometimes mistakes and failures are only temporary delays in reaching your goal. Sometimes mistakes and failures, as hard as they can be, are necessary steps on your road to success. Find value in any failures or mistakes. Failure and mistakes may be the vehicles that bring you closer to success.

Falls are not easy to take. But, accept that they will happen. Study the mistakes and failures of great leaders. Analyze them and what role they played in the leader's eventual success. Do your best to cushion yourself from a fall. Don't hide by staying "safe." Living life fully is an adventure. You will enjoy the wins more than you will be hurt by the falls.

Take the Journey

Sign on for the journey to your own creativity. Start by convincing yourself of the benefits you will gain by being creative versus by staying safe. Many people opt for staying safe. Why? For some, the creative journey seems too risky. Creativity may not be valued in their workplace or market. Group think may seem a lot safer than expressing their own voice. Taking the journey to your own creativity means going within. Some do not want to travel within. They may come up against things they do not like. They may have to change.

What is gained by taking the journey to your own creativity? You will find out who you are. You will bring your unique gifts to your pursuits. You will have a voice that is yours, not someone else's. People will look to you to lead. Many of *The Apprentice* candidates have taken their journey to their own creativity and are continuing on it. Creativity spawns original ideas. Bill Rancic started an Internet cigar business and it made him wealthy. Take a look at what the candidates do after they leave the show. Will they return to the mundane? I doubt it. They will create new steps on their journeys.

Expressing your creativity brings richness to your life. Yes, there may be some places where your creativity is not valued, but you will find or create places where it will be. You will not be trapped in being "safe." How do you take the journey to your own creativity? Take small steps first. Do you consider yourself creative? If not, examine why. How are you defining creativity? Creativity is the expression of who you are. No one else can define that for you.

Once you accept that you are creative, think back to your childhood.

> How did you express who you were?
> What were your creative endeavors?
> Do they have any connection to who you have become?

Then do some experimenting. Try some different things. Maybe you want to write. Maybe you want to build something. Maybe you have a great business idea. Get into expressing your creativity.

> What feels right?
> What do you want to continue?

Look at whether you have the opportunity to be creative in your work. Take some time with this.

> Is someone or something stifling your creativity? Why?
> Are you stifling yourself?
> Identify a creative act you can perform at work. See how it goes.

Taking the journey to your creativity can be fun. Let expressing your creativity become a value in your life. You will join others who are taking the same journey. You will find support and I bet you will enjoy the ride.

Muster the Courage

To think outside the box requires courage. It is no small thing to reveal yourself to the world; to step apart from the crowd. But, you cannot lead without doing it. Think of the courage Bill and Kwame had as they faced their final tasks. They had to work with a team of people who had competed with them and wanted to be where they were. They had to perform under the intense scrutiny of Donald, his staff, the other candidates, and the audience. But they were able to muster the courage. They did it.

Sometimes, I doubt myself. I wonder what it is within me that thinks I can pull something off. When that doubt occurs, I bring up my courage. I tell myself that I do have something to say to the world and that there are people who will want to hear me. I ask myself what purpose I serve by not expressing who I am. We are all free to be true to ourselves. You have something to say to the world and there are people who want to hear you. Don't let someone else create a box around you or your possibilities. Have the courage to look at every situation with your unique perspective.

Nurture Your Creativity

The key to nurturing your creativity is to find your source of inspiration and maintain it. Your source of inspiration is a well to draw from. How will you keep this well full? Your well may be fed by being around people who challenge you in positive ways. Or it may be fed by time alone to ponder and replenish. You may feed it by being with people you love, or you may feed it with ideas. Once you recognize this source, never neglect it.

You may find that work provides enough opportunities to nurture your creativ-

> **Here is a structure for nurturing your creativity that may help you.**
>
> **Value**. Value your creativity. Know its worth to you
>
> **Acknowledge**. Acknowledge that you are a creative being.
>
> **Express**. Keep your creativity alive in the way you live your life and perform your work.
>
> **Protect**. Protect your source of inspiration and feed it often.
>
> **Grow**. Allow your creative expression to grow and expand.

ity. Or, you may have to make an effort to find means of creative expression outside your work. You want to have enough of a source that you can creatively express yourself in your life and the work that you do. Thinking outside the box is only done through the expression of your own creativity.

Nurturing your creativity is a conscious act. You have to focus on it. Creativity can hide itself again easily if you neglect it. Creativity can be beaten down by outside influences if you do not protect it.

Nurturing keeps your creativity alive. Here are some tips to help you nurture your creativity. They are: find the barriers, foster the imagination, see with your own eyes, and express your creativity.

> *"I learned that I could do things I didn't think I could do."*
> —Heidi Bressler

Find the Barriers

What kinds of barriers can inhibit creative expression? There are many. One is social barriers. Our society does not always value true creative expression. Social order depends on group action and harmony. If a society has everyone fully expressing themselves creatively, social order may not be maintained. Clearly, some creative expression exists, but some can also be stifled if it is seen as threatening to the social order.

What about workplace barriers in organizations? In recent years, there has been a lot of discussion regarding the importance of creativity and innovation to business success. But while acknowledging this focus, I question how ready our organizations really are for creativity and innovation.

The need for discipline, order, and hierarchy and resistance to too much change can inhibit creative expression. When someone truly thinks outside the box, it can threaten the order of things. Some organizations are trailblazers in creativity and innovation. But we have a way to go before we can say it is universal. The recent entrepreneurial explosion of small businesses has a lot to do with people's needs for creative expression in their work. Some practices in today's workplace are hindering creativity more than ever before. Downsizing puts great pressures on individual workers. Stress and fatigue stifle creativity. Increased global competition necessitates leaner, more disciplined operations. There isn't always room for creativity. What I call the homogenization of our marketplace also stifles creativity. So many chain stores and fewer local shops are evidence of this.

Here are some questions that may help you identify the barriers to your own creative expression and ability to think outside the box.

> Is creativity valued in your organization or marketplace?
> What happened to your last creative business idea?
> Do you have time to just think?
> What is the source of your inspiration?
> Do you consider yourself creative?
> What ways do you express your creativity?

Foster Your Imagination

This will be fun! In Julia Cameron's *The Artist's Way* she suggests taking an artist's date once a week just to feed the source of your inspiration. What a wonderful suggestion. It gives you time, freedom, and purpose. Your imagination is beautiful. Many great acts have been born within active imaginations. What was your imagination like when you were a child? Think back to that time. Why can't your imagination be that active today?

I know I have been beating up on our social order lately. Society can also inhibit your imagination, as it does your creative expression. But, you have many opportunities to activate your imagination. Even if you cannot at work, find ways to develop a rich imagination. Here are some ideas:

Spend time with children. Watch how they allow their imagination to run free. Encourage yourself to do the same. You don't have to worry about children judging your imaginative expression.

Write or create art. Let yourself go. Pick a medium that is fun for you and create. Imagine things about your workplace. Have fun with it. Imagine you are the CEO. What would you do? What would your organization be like? If you are an entrepreneur, imagine tripling your revenue. What does your organization look like then?

Place value on an active imagination. Nurture it. Even though it may seem that you start out with silly ideas, I think you will be surprised where it leads. As you activate your imagination, it will begin to work for you in very productive ways.

See With Your Own Eyes

Creativity is the expression of your unique view. As you nurture your creativity, make sure to see with your own eyes. Seeing through the eyes of others, keeps you inside the box. Someone has been there already. How far would Donald Trump get if he copied the design of another building in New York? He has his own unique style and vision. Celebrate your individuality. Trust and validate it.

You may have to develop your ability to see with your own eyes. Social interactions and conditionings can blur your vision. Start with some experimenting. Take a situation or object. Describe it to yourself. What do you see? Now, examine how others have seen it. How does their view differ from yours? Try this a few times. Here are some ideas on subjects:

A work of art
A person you work with
A natural scene
A tense situation at work
A movie

As you progress in doing this, add another layer. Examine your descriptions. See how they are influenced by social interactions or conditionings. For example, did a negative or positive review influence your description of a movie? Begin to distill your own unique view out of the mix. Begin to let go of barriers that block your sight.

As you develop your ability to see with your own eyes, you will nurture your creativity. You will see your life and work with your own eyes. It will become easier and easier. It will clear your mind and allow you to think outside the box more and more.

Express Your Creativity

And now we come back to action. To nurture your creativity, express it often. Find ways to be creative-no excuses. If you want to write, start a journal or blog. If you want to be more creative in your work, start doing it. You can even do it retrospectively. For example, look back on a recently completed project. How would you have done the same project if you were thinking outside the box?

Make expression of your creativity a value in your life. Honor it. Find small and large ways to express your creativity. Truly believe you are a creative person. Live creatively. Do not let others criticize or stifle your creativity, and be aware of when that is happening. Get familiar with your own inner judges or critics that stifle your creativity. Identify what they say and when you hear those voices, let them go. Be aware of the limitations our society can put on expressing creativity. When you see a limitation, examine it, understand where it comes from. Do not let it influence your own expression. You are a creative being—believe it.

Expressing your creativity may begin to lead you on a wonderful journey. It can be a lot of fun and has many rewards. You may find your passion. You may find yourself excelling at work. You may find yourself more fulfilled in life. You have nothing to lose. Leaders know how to think outside the box. Expressing your creativity will get you there.

> *"Most of all, listen to your heart and mind*
> *and they will guide you in the right direction."*
> —Diane N. Bark, president of DHB Financial Services, Inc
> quoted in *The Way to the Top*, Donald Trump

Exercise Your Mind

The mind is a focal point for thinking outside the box. I use the word mind assuming you are using it in its full capacity. We tend to put limits on our mind. I speak of mind as an integration of your intellect, your intuition, a source of inspiration, and the parts of the brain that guide your emotions and the functions of your body. It is in this wholeness, that you can use your mind to its full capacity.

What do you think your mind is? Is it a calculator? A synthesizer? A tool? Do you need to expand your concept of mind? And where does knowledge fit in? To think outside the box, start examining the role your mind plays in your life. It is an important creative tool. It is well known that people do not use their brain to its full capacity. Many people limit the mind as a tool by making it a repository for chatter, stress, and fear.

Understanding your mind and how you use it, will help you. Developing your mind and aligning your thoughts and your actions will go far in helping you think outside the box. You are taking your mind to the gym. You are making it fit. Here are some ways to exercise your mind. They are: get rid of mind chatter and clutter, focus on the present moment, stimulate your mind, and live life fully.

Get Rid of Mind Chatter and Clutter

As I grew up and became an adult, my mind was always going. Much of it, I thought, was natural. I also attributed it to growing up in New York City with its fast pace. One task that helped me in developing my creativity was to spend twenty minutes at the end of the day in silence, meditating. By this time I had moved to Los Angeles and my pace was not as fast as in New York. So, twenty minutes of silence? What a joke! Each evening I would go outside, look at the stars, and my mind would chatter away. I couldn't even close my eyes. For the first year, I usually lasted about five minutes and my mind chattered through it all. As thoughts came into my brain, I tried not to push them away, but let them flow right through and then get quiet again. Eventually, my mind began to quiet. I was able to close my eyes and stay outside for twenty minutes. Wow!

My twenty minutes at the end of each day became a contrast with the rest of my life. I began to see how much chatter and clutter occurred within my mind each day. I wanted to change this. I began to find quiet moments within each day when I could center. I started listening to the chatter and realized how useless it was. I realized how I cluttered my brain with stress, anxiety, worries, and what we call "gremlins" in coaching. Gremlins are those inner voices and critics that sabotage us. Your gremlin could be perfectionism, doubt, worry, the judge, the inner critic, or the naysayer. I had a few. I began to observe them and how they held me back. I tried to quiet them, countering with my own affirmative statements each time they spoke.

Gradually my mind began to quiet. What a difference. My thoughts were clearer. Stress was not taking as big a toll. I still work at this often. But now, my mind does not hold as much stress and worry. It is an ally in my life's purpose. It is a valuable tool that, instead of holding me back, moves me forward.

Focus on the Present Moment

As I worked on quieting my mind, my focus turned to living in the present moment. Lynn Andrews said to me if you live in the past, you live in depression. If you live in the future you live in anxiety. The only place where you are fully alive is in the present moment. I have found

How can you focus on the present moment?

Start by asking these questions:

When you are performing a task, are you fully focused on that task?

When you are talking with someone, is your mind on that conversation or is it wandering to something else that has to get done?

How often do you try to do multiple things at one time and do none of them well?

How many times does your mind wander to the past or future, when something needs to be done in the present?

such wisdom in this concept. Focusing on the present moment is a wonderful exercise for your mind. It brings the alignment of your thoughts and actions.

Focusing on the present moment does not mean putting the past or future out of your life. They each have their place. Focusing on the present moment means bringing your full attention to the task at hand. Say, for example, you have a list of ten tasks that must be completed in a day. You receive a call adding two more tasks that must get done right away. This has caused major stress as you don't know how you will get it all done. You find yourself worried, frazzled; you begin to drop things clumsily, and are having difficulty concentrating. If you continue in this state, chances are slim that you will get things done.

Instead what if, as soon as you see the signs of your anxiety, you stop, regroup and bring yourself to the reality of the present moment? You assess the likelihood of completing all the tasks. If necessary, you prioritize them. You identify what you need to proceed. If you decide there just is not time to complete the tasks, call those who are counting on you and tell them when the tasks will be done. Then, focus fully on each task, eliminating distractions and worry. If you try this, I think you will be amazed at how much you are able to complete. By letting go of stress and anxiety and bringing your full attention to the task at hand, things move smoothly and you get the tasks done.

Try this from a positive place. Take a task you are looking forward to doing. Promise yourself that you will give that task your full attention. Eliminate any distractions and begin it. If an unavoidable interruption occurs, handle it and then return to your task. Once completed, examine how you felt while doing the task, the quality of the work you did, and how much time it took. Is there a difference from other times when you tried to complete tasks without giving your full attention? Focusing on the present moment frees you. It allows you to focus on what is occurring now. It aligns your abilities and your senses to the task at hand. It puts you in a flow of energy that moves with you, rather than against you.

Stimulate Your Mind

What stimulates your mind? Some answers for me are: beauty, nature, solitude, new ideas, travel, reading, Book TV, and challenges. Get familiar with what stimulates your mind. Make sure those things are part of your life. There are many demands on your time. But, it is well worth it to find time for this. Think of the variety of tasks *The Apprentice* candidates face. Their minds have to be nimble to think outside the box and figure out the creative approaches that will lead them to a win. Your mind needs stimulation. You cannot fill it with the routine and humdrum and then ask it to work for you in creative ways.

I have a good friend, a lawyer, who uses jigsaw puzzles as one way to keep her mind nimble. She believes that in order to think outside the box, you have to stimulate both your right and left brains. She has plenty to stimulate her left brain as she goes about her life. The left brain tends to take over whenever words are involved. The puzzles are a pure right brain exercise. There are no words. It is a nonverbal task. It is about color and shape and that is right brain.

There is a great product called "The Creative Whack Pack" developed by Roger von Oech. It is a pack of cards that encourage you to think creatively. Find tools and activities and exercises like this that stimulate your mind. Have fun with it!

> *"Deals are my art form."*
> —Donald Trump in *The Art of the Deal*

Live Life Fully

My father often said that one of the best things you can give your children is a sense of curiosity. If you are curious, there is always stimulation. There are things to explore and adventures to embark on. You will not get bored with life. Living life fully expands your horizons. You have many experiences to draw on. To think outside the box you need an active and creative mind.

You can live life fully both within and without. A rich outer life can come from travel, intellectual challenges, a diversity of experiences, interactions with people, or activities that stretch you. A rich inner life can come from contemplation, intellectual pursuits, solitude, writing, or art.

>How can you live your life more fully?
>What can you add to your life?
>What is pulling you down, that you can let go of?
>Should you apply to be a candidate on *The Apprentice*?
>Should you take that trip you've always dreamed of—now?

It is true that the mind is a terrible thing to waste. Use your mind fully. Align it with your body and emotions. Use both your right and left brains and your mind will be a valuable tool as you think outside the box.

Be a Step Ahead

In the first season of *The Apprentice* the men and women were on separate teams for the first four tasks. The women ran away with all four wins; they were always a step ahead. In the first task, selling lemonade, they had a better location, used their feminine wiles, and more than quadrupled the initial investment.

In the second task, developing an ad campaign, the women were the only ones to meet with their client and they developed an edgier campaign.

In the third task, negotiating for a group of items at less than retail cost, the women were much more successful in their negotiating.

In the fourth task managing a shift at a Planet Hollywood restaurant, the women focused their efforts on increasing the bar tab and won again. The women were always a step ahead of the men.

What does being a step ahead have to do with thinking outside the box? If your mind is agile and fast, you'll think of winning strategies before your competition. If you can stay a step ahead, you have a distinct advantage as you think outside the box. Many great ideas are winners because of timing. Their inventors thought of the idea first. They were first to step outside the box and they won.

How can you be a step ahead? Here are some ideas to help you find the answer. They are: develop your endurance, sprint when you have to, value innovation, and stay in touch.

Develop Your Endurance

You want to be a step ahead for the long run, so you must develop endurance. Your endurance depends on a number of factors. The most important is to maintain balance as we discussed in Chapter Five. You have to be physically, emotionally, spiritually, and mentally fit to stay ahead. If you are not, you will lose momentum and your ability to endure. You must also have commitment. Is it important to you that you remain a step ahead? If so, it will take time and effort. How will you know you are a step ahead? You have to keep up with what is happening in your field—trends, advances, and the like. You have to believe in yourself; that you have what it takes to endure and you have something unique to offer the world.

Why does endurance matter? Because you want to be a step ahead for the long run. I have seen examples of innovators who have had one good idea in their careers. At a certain point, if new ideas are not coming, they start to "milk" their first idea. It doesn't work. Times and conditions change. Their first idea no longer applies and eventually, they are out of the game. They have not endured; they are no longer a step ahead.

Donald Trump has endurance. He has had many different ventures. Some have made it; some have failed. But he is still a player. He can adapt to new playing fields. He believes in himself. He needed a lot more than his first real estate idea to make a success of *The Apprentice*. His endurance keeps him on the playing field over the long run and brings him to new playing fields and new successes.

Sprint When You Have To

Sometimes you have to sprint to stay ahead. Let's say a key market condition changes in your field. You have to respond quickly in order to stay ahead of the competition. How can you build your ability to sprint when you have to? Develop your agility. Accept that change will happen and learn to respond quickly.

When I ran New York City's Hazardous Materials Emergency Response Team, developing agility was critical to my ability to do the job. We responded to over six hundred chemical emergencies a year. My first notice was the emergency call from a member of the team. Often, at that point we had few details, but we had to respond now. As a team, we had to read a situation quickly. Misjudgments could have serious consequences. We had to make decisions on next steps with insufficient information, in most cases. We had to make decisions with the best interests of the city in mind. All emergency teams develop agility. They have instant communication, processes to quickly size up a situation, and people who thrive in fast environments.

On an ongoing basis, have in place what you will need the next time you have to sprint. Be in balance. Have a team that works well together. Keep in touch with what your competition is doing. When you know you have to sprint, get started, and make any adjustments you need to. Keep your focus on the endpoint, making sure someone is watching over anything that you are not. Know what to do when the sprint is over to recover and stay in the longer race.

You don't want to focus on endurance alone and then watch the competition sprint past you. Your ability to sprint can help you stay a step ahead.

Value Innovation

Innovation is not a once-in-awhile thing; it is a frame of mind. Make it one of your values. Innovation is the introduction of something new; it is an engine that can help you think outside the box. Innovate is an active verb. You have to keep your mind alert and alive to innovate. What opportunities do you have to innovate in your work right now?

Innovation involves imagining what is possible. Then, to make it happen, you find the steps that will get you there. Sometimes it takes courage to innovate. By its very nature, innovation goes against the norm. Innovation often involves risk. But, people and companies that value innovation are usually a step ahead. How can you make innovation a part of your world? First, value the creative process and whatever it takes to support it. Second, convince yourself that the investment of time and money involved in innovation is worth it. Third, accept that there is always risk in innovation. You cannot have absolute certainty and innovate.

Are you innovating in your life right now? If not, why not? Make innovation a value. Let it be a part of your strategy to look for opportunities to innovate. Give yourself what you need to become an innovator.

Stay in Touch

No, this is not a phone company commercial. By staying in touch, I mean know what is going on around you. This allows you to know the playing field and what you have to stay ahead of. With all the demands on your time, staying in touch takes strong focus and intent. You can stay in touch by networking with people in your field. You can stay in touch by reading about what is happening in the business world. You can keep up with what trendsetters and innovators are doing. You cannot stay in a small world and get what you need to innovate.

RECAP

Forget "safe." Leaders are willing to push the edge of the envelope.

Nurture your creativity. Find and maintain the source of your inspiration.

Exercise your mind. Stay actively creative and think beyond the norm.

Be a step ahead. Keep in front of the competition.

EXERCISES

1. Explore focusing on the present moment by not doing it! Purposely, plan to do two things at once. (For example, wash the car while speaking on the phone.) Do them both. How did it go? Were there times you were distracted? How was the quality of each thing you did? How efficiently was your time used?

2. Identify the barriers to your creativity. Begin a creative project. See what comes up to thwart you in the project. Write down any inner voices, outside influences, confidence breakers, doubts, or challenges that come up.

3. Do something this week, that you do not think is safe. Don't put yourself in any danger—do something that you define as pushing the envelope. See how it goes. How did you feel? What did you learn?

CHAPTER EIGHT
LESSON SEVEN: KNOW WHEN TO JOIN AND WHEN TO LEAD

"All I said was I think we were duped." —Tammy Lee

As the Versacorp team sat in the boardroom with Donald, they explained their loss. Katrina, project manager for Versacorp, said Troy, project manager for Protégé, had been unethical in the way he negotiated with her at the beginning of the task. Donald disagreed. He thought Katrina was duped by Troy. Katrina's team members backed her up. All excluding Tammy, who said she thought they had been duped. Later, in the boardroom, Donald gave his views on what went wrong in the task. But task performance did not lead to that week's firing. Donald thought that Tammy's disloyalty was so egregious that he fired her!

Why Tammy made that choice, I do not know. But Donald's view is clear. There are times to join and times to lead. In this instance, Donald was looking for Tammy to be part of her team, even though in the bigger picture, he was looking for an apprentice who was a leader. As you develop your leadership abilities, pay attention to when to join and when to lead. A leader isn't always leading. A leader is often part of a team. A leader can inspire loyalty and contribute to the success of their team by knowing how to work well with them.

This is a delicate dance. It involves maintaining your presence as a leader but also having the ability to work as part of a team. Sometimes you will be leading a team and sometimes you won't. There are different styles of leadership. Some leaders always maintain a distance from their team. They may believe it is important to set themselves apart. They may believe their effectiveness as a leader depends on this distance. They may believe that they must be better than their team to be its leader. Other leaders become part of their teams. They maintain their role as leader, but can pitch in and help get the job done. They see themselves as a contributing member of a team, as well as a leader. Sometimes, as on *The Apprentice,* you may find yourself in a situation where at different times, you are team leader and team member. Knowing when to join and when to lead is a factor in your success as a leader.

How do you respond as a team member to these styles of leadership? Do you like a leader to keep a distance or to pitch in? Personally, I have always responded best to leaders who are part of the team. It takes a special kind of leader to do this. They must know how to gain and keep the respect of their team, while being part of them. Have you known leaders like this? I do not always respond well to leaders who set themselves apart. I value relationship. I also do not see myself or other leaders as above, or as better than others. I respect people who lead me and follow their lead. But, I value dialogue and want them to value my contribution as a team member.

How do you, as a leader, want to handle the delicate dance of when to join and when to lead? Here are some questions to ask yourself.

> What is the overall role of a leader?
> What is your natural personal style?
> What kind of interaction with team members is most effective for getting the job done?
> How do you handle being a member of a team under another leader?
> How do you view the role of the members of your team?

Is a leader innately superior to the members of a team?
Where does loyalty come into play for both leaders and team members?
How does a leader gain and retain the respect of their team?
What is the role of team members?
What do team members owe their leaders?
What do leaders owe their team members?

Knowing when to join and when to lead will help you develop your leadership style. Leaders have to lead. They can lead alone in some cases. When they have a project that needs a team, the dance of knowing when to join and when to lead becomes important. Here are some concepts that will help you dance.

Be a Team Player

What does it mean to be part of a team? A team works together. Whether they do it effectively or not has a lot to do with their leader. What if you are leader of the team? How do you want the team to function? What are the components of your team? What differentiation do you want to establish between you as leader and your team members? You can be a team player and a leader at the same time.

Let's take a look at Donald Trump. Admittedly, I am looking from afar. But I discerned some things about his leadership style that apply here. Donald appeared to respect his managers, George Ross and Carolyn Kepcher. He trusted them to observe the candidates and bring information back to him. He wanted their input when he faced the decision of who to fire.

When the field of candidates narrowed, Donald brought in senior managers from his organization to interview the candidates. He wanted to assure that the person chosen as The Apprentice would fit in and have the respect of his management team. In the interviews, some of his managers were not impressed with Amy. Although Donald thought highly of Amy and believed she had done the best of the candidates until then, he trusted his people. He fired Amy saying, without the respect of his managers, it would be hard to bring her into his team. I think here that Donald saw himself as part of a team. He is undeniably its leader, but he joined his managers as he made his decision on who would be his apprentice.

How can you be a team player, but also lead? When I worked for the City of New York and managed its hazardous materials response team, I had to find an answer to this question. The "haz mat" team was a group of highly skilled scientists and engineers. In serious situations involving hazardous chemicals and the health and safety of New Yorkers, others and I relied on their expertise in making our decisions. Not a scientist or engineer myself, I had to hire people whose expertise and judgment I respected. When it came to making decisions, we made them together. As a team we came to an understanding of our respective roles and of each other. I think we functioned well together. My role as leader was not compromised. They were respected for the professionals they were. As others relied on us, we came across as a coherent team that knew what we were doing.

Learning how to be a team player is a key element of developing as a leader. Here are some things to consider as you learn. They are: be yourself, set an agenda, understand people, and foster productivity.

Be Yourself

We spent a lot of time in Chapter Three on the value of being yourself. It applies here as well. True leaders are genuine. People see them as the real thing. Leaders with false pretenses are not respected and are soon found out. Being yourself is your own, unique journey. You may admire others and want to emulate them. That is good. But, your leadership style has to be true to who you are.

As a leader, it is important to have the trust of those around you. How do you win their trust? People want to know who their leaders are, what motivates them, and how they want to lead. As a leader, reveal who you are to those you lead. Let them know your philosophy of leadership and how you want to work with them. Let them know what your expectations are, of yourself and of them. It is not warranted to let them know intimate details of your life. They are getting to know you as a leader. It is who you are as a leader that matters.

Establish your style as a leader. This helps you know yourself as well as let others know how to work with you. Inconsistency in your leadership style doesn't work. People do not know how to work with you. Have you ever worked with people who are inconsistent? It can be very disconcerting. You find a way of working with them and then suddenly the playing field is different. They can be communicative one day and incommunicative the next. You are given one set of directions and then mid-stream the directions change. If your team knows how you want to work, they can flow with your style and let you know how they fit into it. What is your leadership style? Here are some questions to get you started.

> Do you see yourself as a guide for your team or as a director?
> How much control do you want of what your team does?
> How do you like to communicate with your team?
> What will you give to your team?
> What do you expect of your team?
> How independent do you want your team members to be?
> What personalities do you work best with?
> Do you prefer consensus or competition?
> How much direction do you want to give your team?
> How do you expect your team to work together?

In Chapter Three we also talked about knowing your values. This is worthwhile to look at from the perspective of leadership. What are your values as a leader? Here are some areas within which to explore your values: interaction of leader and team, how to get the job done, quality of work, what defines a win, and ethics of a team. In each of these areas, what are your values? What other values can you identify? Knowing and communicating your values can go a long way in building a strong team.

Set an Agenda

To lead effectively, you must set an agenda. An agenda, as used it here, goes beyond having a plan. On a broad scale, your agenda is your point of view regarding leading your team and accomplishing your project goals. In leading your team your values, your style, and your vision comprise your agenda. In accomplishing your project goals, your plan, your timeline, and your systems comprise your agenda. Your agenda must guide the work of your team at all times and be communicated clearly to your team members.

On *The Apprentice*, Donald sets the initial agenda in the dossier for each project. In the dossier he provides the team with the objective and the rules. Once the team receives the dossier, they set the agenda for accomplishing the objective. It is clear from the beginning what is to be accomplished, the means to do it, and the timing. Having an agenda maximizes the efficiency and effectiveness of the team—everyone is on the same page. The goals are set and communicated. The team knows the leader's vision and how he or she wants to manage the project.

Without an agenda, the team will flounder. Team members may be working at cross-purposes. Methods and goals may not be clear. Communication may not be effective. It is like steering a ship without navigation tools.

Understand People

Great leaders understand people. They spend time getting to know the members of their team. They observe people and some study human nature. And, they learn how to manage people and create winning outcomes for everyone involved.

As a leader, you are often dependent on people to get a job done. It makes sense to understand people and what makes them tick so that you can give them what they need to succeed. It also makes sense to understand people so that you can know what types of people you need on your team.

Many people overlook this. They think that the goal is almighty and people are only tools. They think money can buy anything they need. They go for a win at any cost, leaving people in their wake. They think only of themselves and do not acknowledge the role other people play in their success, but they do this at their own risk. If a leader does not earn the trust of others, eventually they are doomed. If a leader does not understand people, they are at risk of making costly, time-consuming mistakes by having unrealistic expectations.

As you assemble your team, give some thought not only to the skills you need in team members, but also to the kinds of people you need to succeed. Set a vision of what your team will be. What personal qualities in its members will allow your team to work the way you want it to? Do you want cooperative people, competitive people, independent people, team-oriented people? Sometimes you cannot choose the people on your team. In that case, make your expectations clear. Set the way the team will work together. Communicate your values.

Once your team is assembled, provide what team members need to do their best and succeed. Give them the resources and tools they need. Provide an environment that is conducive for the work they have to do. Keep in communication with them, then focus on individual team members, or in a larger project, your key managers. Ask them individually what they need to perform and do your best to provide it. Create a means for them to let you know on a regular basis if new needs arise.

In many organizations understanding people involves understanding cultural differences. You and your team members must have awareness of cultural points of view and mores in order to work together effectively. Without this understanding, conflicts can arise that could have easily been avoided. Cultural differences can be accommodated without hampering the success of a project. It may take some time, but it is well worth it.

You can go deeper into this by understanding what motivates your team—as a whole and individually. Motivators can vary. Some are motivated by acknowledgement; others by money. Seeing progress motivates some. Having the opportunity to work independently motivates some, while being part of a team motivates others. It is reality that you may not be able to accommodate all motivating factors. But making an effort to understand them is well worth it. As opportunities arise to motivate your people you will recognize them.

> "The American dream is still alive and well,
> and nice guys can finish first."
> —Bill Rancic

Foster Productivity

You want a productive team. How can you get there? Here are some suggestions.

Develop Clear Measures

We often hear that you manage what you measure. This is true for leaders who want to succeed. You can develop measures for yourself, individuals and your team. Measures foster productivity by giving team members a clear explanation of what you expect. Measures must be reinforced and tallied. Staff meetings should include progress reports on individual members. Meetings should be held with individual team members on their progress against their measures.

Have an Open Door

Communication must be free and open if you are to succeed. This is not an invitation to bedlam, but rather a philosophy. Make yourself available. Let issues and problems rise that need your attention. Let team members know that what they have to say counts. There are many ways to have an open door. It can be a general policy that your door is always open. You can establish specific hours on a frequent basis that you are available outside of scheduled meetings. You can develop a system for issues or problems to be raised to your attention. You can hold forums for open communication with your team.

Recognition

Acknowledgement goes a long way. Design solid mechanisms by which you recognize your team. You can do it in a short, written note on a document they submitted to you. You can do it in conversation. You can recognize someone in front of the group, or you can recognize them individually. You can conduct meetings to review progress and acknowledge what has been accomplished.

Rewards

Rewards take recognition a step further. Develop meaningful rewards for good work. One company I consulted to had a catalog of merchandise that could be bought through a point system. When teams met their safety goals, they would receive points. A certain number of points bought merchandise in the catalog. Rewards can be monetary bonuses, certificates, plaques, or anything you want. Use your imagination. Give rewards in a meaningful way. Do not overdo it. A reward is given for exceptional performance.

Think for Yourself

Whether you are working alone or as part of a team, always think for yourself. You are the center of your universe. No one else can see the world through your eyes. Others can help or influence you, but ultimately you make the decisions. I talk with my clients often about giving away your power to other people. There are many ways to do this. You can convince yourself that someone has control over you. You can believe you do not have choice in a situation. You can believe you are powerless.

You have power in every situation. It is possible that you may not have all the options you'd like to or other factors may have influence with you. But, you hold the reins for your life. You make the decisions.

Acknowledging your power comes with responsibilities. You are accountable for the decisions you make. You have to stand up in difficult situations and sometimes face adversity. Therein lies your power. You live your life, no one else. Many times people give away their power because it is the easier thing to do. Some people resign themselves that they cannot live the life they want. Others fall into a victim mentality. They believe the circumstances of their life are beyond their ability to control. But, if you acknowledge your power in every situation and accept its responsibilities, you will be able to move your life forward.

If you think for yourself you will know when to join and when to lead. At times you will decide to act on your own. Other times you will decide it is best to be part of a team. Sometimes this decision is clear-cut. Sometimes it involves hard choices.

Tammy decided to act on her own, apart from the team and it hurt her. When Troy and Kwame—who had become good friends—ended up in the boardroom together, we saw an example of a hard choice to act alone. Troy was project manager and chose Kwame to face Donald in the boardroom. He said Kwame never really shined. Troy had decided to lead.

As a leader, you must always think for yourself. You must know when to join and when to lead. Here are some factors in thinking for yourself. They are: discernment, the plusses of thinking for yourself, the challenges of thinking for yourself, and getting good at it.

Discernment

Discernment is the ability to comprehend what is obscure. It is not always easy to determine when to join or when to lead. How do you develop discernment? I think it is learned by practice. First, bring your awareness to your ability to discern whether to join or lead. Here are some methods you can use.

Observe

Observe situations where you or others have to discern whether to join or lead. Look at the particulars of the situation. Is there a clear-cut choice? Or, is the choice harder to see? What are the potential benefits and consequences of each choice? Then, observe what happens when the choice is made. How does it turn out? Who is affected? Is the desired outcome reached?

Recognize

Recognize when you have a choice to join or lead. Do not give away your power.

Experiment

Create experiments. In your everyday life, make varying choices whether to join or lead. See what results from your choices. Are you discerning correctly? If not, what did you miss-a consequence, someone fighting back, an unanticipated difficulty? If you are, what did you do right?

Develop

Develop your skill at discernment. It will serve you well in the future. There are various factors that can cloud your ability to discern. The stress of a situation can diminish your mental acuity. Your emotions can cloud your judgment. You can be giving away your power in small or large ways. You can be unfamiliar with a situation you are in. You can be up against a powerful argument or opponent. You can have a lot at risk. Be aware of these factors and learn to recognize them. Eventually you will be able to handle them and will strengthen your ability to discern.

The Plusses of Thinking for Yourself

One of the big plusses of thinking for yourself is that you will be guiding your life. This is no small advantage. You guide your life towards your definition of success. Guiding your life brings fulfillment. You are not at the mercy of others. You are not doing things that go against your essential nature. As you think for yourself, you will begin to distinguish yourself as an individual. You will get to know yourself. Others will get to know you. You are not draining your energy by always reacting to others.

Thinking for yourself defines you. People will begin to notice you. Donald Trump clearly thinks for himself. He has created a unique brand. He approaches his projects the way he wants to. People admire and respect him for it. As you think for yourself, your creativity will grow. Your ideas are unique and will no longer be clouded by others. You will gain energy. You will be your own source of energy as you grow and develop. You will begin to have fun. We are meant to create our own identity in the world and to express it. New opportunities will appear. People will be able to recognize what is unique about you.

Thinking for yourself brings clarity. You will know who you are and what you want. Choices will become clearer through this lens. You may even see conflicts diminish in their intensity. If you are thinking for yourself, you can state your position clearly for others. You will not be easily drawn into their dramas and complications.

> *"Honesty. Integrity. First, last, always."*
> —Lloyd L. Hill, chairman and CEO, Applebee's International, Inc.
> quoted in *The Way to the Top*, Donald Trump

The Challenges of Thinking for Yourself

I believe the main challenge you face in thinking for yourself is that you are alone. You set yourself apart. You take on the responsibilities of your choices. You have to create your own safety net. When I left my company to become a coach, our office manager said that, as I jumped off the cliff, she hoped I landed in a bed of feathers. As I jumped, I had to accept that whatever happened was my doing.

Our society creates shelter for us. If you go along with society's dictates, it protects you. It gives you a blueprint for life, it sets a structure; it lessens your risk. Things can still go wrong, but you find comfort and validation in numbers. Sometimes society can discourage you from thinking for yourself. When you go it alone, society's cushion can disappear. You experience the consequences of your choices. You can be wrong and you are left looking at yourself.

Another challenge is that it may take time to develop your ability to think for yourself. Much will be pushing against you. You may be uncomfortable with the solitude. You may lose your sense of safety, until you develop it for yourself. You may make some undesirable choices. You have to develop faith in yourself.

You might decide to go at it slowly. You will not see results right away. Your commitment will help you get through this time. Keep in mind the plusses of thinking for yourself and how they will improve your life.

Getting Good at it

As you get comfortable thinking for yourself, the challenges will ease. You will find a stride, and clarity will develop. Your leadership abilities will define themselves. People will recognize your gifts. Your reliance on social dictates will lessen. As I began to think for myself, my stress level decreased. Others did not pull me in so many directions, and I did not get caught up in others' dramas. What I wanted became clearer. I began to say no to situations that drained my energy.

Thinking for myself, I could not find good reasons to put up with bad situations. I became more focused. I knew where I wanted to go, and the steps to get there were revealed. If something didn't fit in, I knew it. I had more time and less distraction. I began to recognize what was unique about me. I had my own voice and spoke it, and could recognize when others were trying to control me, or not acting in my interest. I could remove myself from unhealthy situations quickly and gracefully.

Thinking for yourself is essential to effective leadership. Can you imagine a leader that has to rely on others in order to make a decision? Can you imagine a leader who gives away their power? Your ability to think for yourself will enrich your life. As you get good at it, I think you will find yourself rising. You are meant to live your own life. There is a place for you in the world-a good place. Thinking for yourself will help you find it.

Self-Serving Doesn't Work

I may be going against the grain here, but I believe that self-serving doesn't work. The approach has its limits—in the long run it backfires. Self-serving leaders are found out; people do not trust them. They tire of them. By self-serving I mean a total focus on your own interests to the exclusion of others'. Self-serving leaders disregard and disrespect others; they do not see the merits of individuals. They can use their skills to dominate or manipulate others. Our society involves a lot of interaction. To get your work done, you often rely on others. If you do not show others the same respect you want, they will grow to resent you. Then, how will you get your work done?

As you develop your ability to know when to join and when to lead, learn how to consider the interests of others along with your own. Consideration of others does not diminish you. It enhances you as a leader. In the past few years, more focus has been put on self-serving leaders. I have read articles about "bully bosses," people feeling betrayed at work, the stress caused by negativity at work, and people who are angry at work. These articles discuss the harmful effects self-serving leaders create. People are being encouraged not to stand for it. Gradually, people are deciding that they do not need to put up with it. They can go somewhere else. Self-serving leaders may soon find themselves alone.

Here are some things I have learned about self-serving leaders. They are: types of self-serving people, the difference between self-serving and a sense of self worth, what to do with a self-serving colleague, and acting with the interests of others in mind.

Types of Self-Serving People

Learn to recognize self-serving people. Here are some types that I have encountered. They are self-serving because they put their interests above all others and serving their interests can harm the people around them. Have you encountered these types of people? What have you observed about them? What have you done when they negatively affected you?

Creating Chaos

This type of person thrives on disorder, confusion, and turmoil. He creates chaos in his own sphere and in his interactions with others. There are many variations of this. For example, the boss who is always too frantic and busy to discuss things that are important to you, the coworker who can't find the information you need for your project, or the person who gets out of assignments because management thinks they are too frazzled to get it done. Others create chaos by generating situations to draw others in. For example, the coworker who can't handle a broken copier and draws the whole office into the problem.

How does it serve a person to create chaos? For some, it puts attention directly on them, for others, it is a means of avoiding a conversation or work assignment they don't want to have, and for still others, control is gained through chaos, by setting others off balance. Chaos can also be a state of being for a person without a specific intent in the workplace. Because of their internal makeup, they may not be able to find order in their work.

Displaying Anger

This type of person frequently expresses anger. His anger can show itself through outbursts, mean-spiritedness, or other negative interactions. This anger can be very unsettling to those who encounter it, and can be intimidating, hurtful, or disarming. It is a palpable energy. Imagine the tension in a room after the angry outburst of a boss.

How does it serve a person to express their anger? He may not care about the effect his anger has on others. Expressing his anger may be a release for him, a way to be rid of internal negative energy. Others may use their anger to gain power over others, to cause people to be "careful around them." As with chaos, anger can be a state of being with no specific intent.

Manipulating for Self-Gain

This type of person thrives on the game. She holds hidden agendas to get where she wants to go. People are pawns. She can have any kind of exterior, pleasant, smooth, or angry. Her energy lies underneath, in her plans and scheming. She can use people and situations to get what he wants. She puts massive effort into reading situations and finding just how to get her way. Hiding her motives is essential, in her view.

How does it serve people to be manipulators? It's simple: they believe it is how they will get what they want. Somewhere along the line they were taught this; by a hard lesson or the mentoring of another manipulator. Some may love the game itself and feed off it. For others, it may be a way to diminish other people, feeding an internal need. They may believe it is the only way for them to succeed.

Seeking Control

This type of person arranges her work life to assure she has control over others. She can do this in a myriad of ways: by inspiring dependency from others, by diminishing others to lower their self esteem, by intimidation or by excelling in their work to get on top. Controllers can be subtle or obvious; what matters is the end result. This type of energy tends to work for a while, but often is an illusion and results in a sense of distrust or outright rebellion from others. Then, the person will move on in one form or another to find another environment that gives her a sense of control.

How does it serve a person to seek control of others? For many, their point of view is that they must control others to survive. If they have control, their work life is predictable. By controlling others, they gain something—security, satisfaction, a sense of being needed. For many, this need for control traces directly back to situations where they felt insecure and had no control. Gaining control allows them to endure.

The Difference Between Self-Serving and a Sense of Self Worth

A sense of self worth is a belief that you deserve and can create a meaningful life. We have discussed that self-serving is about putting your interests first to the detriment of others.

Spend some time thinking about the difference between self-serving and self worth. It is an important distinction. Self-serving leadership clouds your ability to know when to join and when to lead. You focus only on serving yourself. You will not have the trust of those around you. Sometimes it is in your own interest to give consideration to the interests of others.

Develop your sense of self worth. Any candidate for *The Apprentice* needs a sense of self worth to win. They must believe in themselves and their abilities. They must be able to convince others that they have what it takes. They must believe in their ability to perform. Can you imagine the confidence it takes to convince Donald Trump that you can win? Donald demands it. If a candidate is self-serving, they will not last. They will lose the respect and trust of others. They will not be able to work well with a team. Donald appears to value teamwork as well as individuality.

> Think about yourself.
> Are you self-serving?
> Do you have a sense of self worth?
> How do your answers define your leadership style?
> Is there anything you want to change?

Self Worth

You believe in yourself
You value yourself
You have strength
You know your skills
You have confidence

Self-Serving

You put your interests above others

Serving your interests can hurt others

Your interests depend on controlling or manipulating others

You do not value others

What to Do With a Self-Serving Colleague

You're going to run up against self-serving colleagues, count on it. Here are some strategies should you encounter a self-serving colleague.

> First, study them. Observe and analyze as best you can, where they are coming from.
> What characterizes their self-serving interest?
> Are they angry, manipulating, controlling, or something else?
> How do they get what they want?
> How do they treat people?
> How do people respond to them?
> What do you think their agenda is?
> Then look carefully at how they are interacting with you.
> How are they treating you?
> How do you think they see you?
> What do they want from you—or how do they think you can serve their interests?
> What are they doing, that makes you think they are self-serving?

> Once you have a sense of them, analyze your own interests.
> What do you want from the situation?
> How can you communicate what you want to them?
> What do you need to consider—do they have authority over you, can they harm you in some way or make your life difficult?
> Considering their tactics, what is the best way to approach them?
> What choices do you have in the situation?
> Are you willing to fight them for what you want?
> What are you willing to risk?

At some point you must take action. Understanding how this colleague operates and how you react to them, will help you serve your interests. It is not worth it to let a person disregard your interests for their own. You are the best person to defend your interests. Prepare yourself and think out what can happen and what you will do. No matter what the outcome, you will win. A sense of self worth is priceless and will lead you to success.

"A perceived lack of integrity is the death sentence in business."
—Thomas M. Joyce quoted in *The Way to the Top*, Donald Trump

Acting with the Interests of Others in Mind

Whether you decide to join or lead it serves you to act with the interests of others in mind. What you are doing here is balancing your interests with the interests of others. You can come from many starting points. You may have to think a bit less about your own interests and think more of others. You may have to let go of conditionings, for example, that thinking of your interests is selfish. You may have to start putting yourself first.

When I became a manager, I was what you call a people pleaser. I needed the approval of others. That point of view influenced my work. I wanted people to like me, and I went overboard to make the people who worked for me happy—sometimes to the detriment of getting our work done.

When I became Assistant Commissioner of Hazardous Materials in New York City, I knew that had to change. My interests were to succeed and run the program well. I began to see how how my need to please was negatively affecting my work. But, I knew it would not serve others—or me—to swing the pendulum in the opposite direction. I searched for how I could balance my needs, the needs of those who worked for me, and the need to get the job done. I decided to focus on fairness. I would set the goals for our organization, value the input of others, consider the needs of individuals within the context of getting the job done, and set a standard that I be fair. This standard replaced the standard of wanting people to like me.

In putting this standard of fairness into practice, I did several things. I communicated my expectations to the people who worked for me. I listened to what they had to say. I accommodated their needs whenever I could without negatively affecting our work. I respected and valued the people who worked toward our goals. If a problem arose, I tried to communicate effectively to the person involved and let them know what needed to change. When hard decisions had to be made, I used a standard of being fair. I am sure you could talk to some people who worked for me, who may disagree with my interpretation of my actions. But, there are others who recognized my approach and worked well with it. Bottom line was that I found a way to balance my interests with the interests of others.

What is your starting point in leading with the interests of others in mind? How can you balance your needs with those of others? If you do, everyone will win and the job will get done.

RECAP

Be a team player. Moving forward together and getting the job done.
Think for yourself. Know when to act on your own.
Self-serving doesn't work. The limits of a self-serving approach.

EXERCISES

1. List ten elements of your leadership style.

2. Profile a work colleague whom you think is self-serving. In your profile include a description of how he or she interacts with others (e.g.: controlling or manipulating), how they get what they want, what effect they have on you, whether you give away your power to them, and what is the most effective way to deal with them.

3. List three things you can do to improve your ability to discern when to join and when to lead.

CHAPTER NINE
"YOU'RE HIRED!"
WINNING

"Now that I've been fired, I realize he was saying, 'Win this Sam.'"
—Sam Solovey

So, we are at the end of the lessons. What does it all come down to? It comes down to winning. Bill Rancic won the opportunity to become Donald's first Apprentice from the show. This may be a good time for you to look at winning. There is a lot involved in winning. How do you define winning? What are you willing to do to get there? Winning can be many things. I would like to share with you some of my thoughts on winning.

Winning on *The Apprentice*

We see many winning traits on *The Apprentice*. We can start with the seven lessons:

Take Risks
Be Yourself
Know the Game
Maintain Balance
Have a Strategy
Think Outside the Box
Know When to Join and When to Lead

We've spent some time with each of them. All the candidates exhibited these traits in varying degrees. What else does *The Apprentice* teach us about winning?

- In business you usually have to compete to win. This show is built on a foundation of competition—in every episode, someone loses. Every candidate is working to be the last one standing.

- Other people can impact whether you win or lose. Donald, Carolyn, and George all bring their views on winning to the boardroom. Their judgment of candidates' performance matters.

- Sometimes, to win, you must work with what you are dealt. Candidates can't prepare for particular tasks; they have to go with what they get the moment the dossier is given to them.

- Alliances are often part of winning. Alliances occur on the show—tensions do too. These alliances and tensions influence who wins and who loses.

- Sometimes you win and sometimes you lose. Candidates are on winning and losing teams. Losing matters—but you're not down until it's over.

- Outside factors affect whether you win or lose. Market conditions, time constraints, team members, and dealing with customers all affect the candidates' ability to win.

The Apprentice teaches you a lot about winning. You see the rewards and consequences. You see what Donald thinks about winning and what he does with what he has. You see people giving their all to win, and you see why people lose. In the end you see only one Apprentice. That person is the winner.

Men and Women, Winning and Leading

One aspect of the show's first season that fascinated me was the interaction of the men and women. At the start of the show, men and women were competing against each other, and the women ran away with the first four wins. The men were stunned. During their winning streak, Donald and Carolyn warned the women against using their sexuality as their main tool in winning. After the first four wins, Donald changed to coed teams. Of the final four candidates, only one woman, Amy, remained. Amy, although a star performer, was playing a game with Nick using her femininity to some purpose. In interviews, some of Donald's staff saw her as lacking substance and not a person they would want to work with. Why? This didn't add up. How did gender affect the competition?

The women did well in their first four tasks. Although they had tensions among them, they knew how to work as a team, focus, and get things done. They made good calls. They demonstrated skill and business acumen. The women seemed comfortable using their sexuality to win when there was an all-female team. You didn't see much of that once the teams went coed, but that may be a result of Donald and Carolyn's warning. The men took some time getting started and made some poor calls. They didn't seem as comfortable working as a team.

Why did the women show so poorly in the long run? Kristi and Jesse were fired for their passivity. Donald's staff saw Amy as lacking substance, even though she had a winning record. Could they have misread the game they were in? Did the women lose something when they joined the men? Why did Donald make the teams go coed? Why not let the women continue their winning streak? Why did he segregate male and female teams in the first place? Heidi complained that Kwame did not trust her. Katrina complained that Bill did not take her suggestions seriously. It is interesting that Bill and Kwame were the finalists. As far as the show, I am mainly raising questions. I do not know the answers. It would be fascinating to study this and I hope someone does. These are serious questions and it behooves us to pay attention to how men and women lead and win.

We are all aware of the differences between men and women. These differences come into play in business and leadership. I do not think we can stereotype that men lead and win one way and women another. As I began writing this section, my focus was on men and women as separate entities. I soon realized I could not stereotype that the women were this way and the men another. Every one is an individual. Perhaps it is not as much about focusing on gender as it is about masculine and feminine perspective and the balance of the two within each of us.

We each have a masculine and feminine side within. If these two sides are balanced, we are at our best. If they are unbalanced, harmony is gone and things go wrong. Think of the social structures of matriarchy (dominance of the female line) and patriarchy (dominance of the male line). Both social structures worked in their day, but they were not ideal. One perspective dominated the other, resulting in constrained expression of one side. We are in a patriarchal culture that is undergoing change. Those entrenched in the patriarchy are fighting to keep things as they are. Those who feel slighted by the patriarchy are trying to swing the pendulum over to their side. Others are trying to restore a balance between the masculine and feminine. The same principles apply within us. We will work well together when each individual balances their masculine and feminine sides within and understands the differences.

What do I mean by masculine and feminine perspective? In general terms, a masculine perspective is characterized by an outward focus. Masculine perspective brings force to our endeavors. There is a clarity in this perspective. Mind and knowledge are key factors. A feminine perspective is characterized by a receptive focus. Feminine perspective brings creativity to our endeavors. There are strong intuitive abilities.

There is a need for balancing masculine and feminine energies. I work to be aware of when I am carrying a "male" shield and when I am carrying a "female" shield. By doing this, I can see the difference between the two. I observe when the female shield is most effective and when the male is. Through this exercise, I can balance my own feminine and masculine sides within. It has made a big difference in my life. I know better when to bring force to a situation and when to bring receptivity. I better understand the masculine side. I can see when others are carrying a male or female shield and deal with them accordingly.

So how do I bring this back to men and women winning and leading on *The Apprentice* and in life? Thinking of the women's winning streak, the women had all succeeded in a patriarchal business world. My guess is that their masculine sides were well developed. They certainly have developed their feminine sides. Perhaps it was the right balance of masculine and feminine that won. If we shift our focus to the attributes of masculine and feminine perspectives, we move away from dividing men and women. It is not that we are separate. The present imbalance is caused by socialization—a patriarchal system that does not always value the feminine. Rebalancing can come from valuing masculine and feminine perspectives equally and putting our values into practice. What do you think?

The Importance of Fair Play

In winning, fair play matters. The only competition worth winning is on a fair playing field. What do I mean by fair? I mean that in winning you have honored your values. You have respected the right of the competition to be there. You are not deceptive or dishonest. Notice that I did not say an even playing field. People come to competition with their differences. You can take advantage of these differences. You can build a strategy around your strong points and exploit the competition's weak ones. *The Apprentice* set up a fair playing field. The rules were clear. How to win was specified. I saw no examples of egregious deception or dishonesty. Everyone played to win.

Not all playing fields are as structured as that of *The Apprentice*. Sometimes you don't know all the players. Sometimes the rules aren't clear. This gives you all the more reason to honor your values as you play. As you lead, keep fair play in mind. Here are some things to consider as you do.

Act with integrity
Be honest
Be ethical
Respect personal boundaries
Treat people as you want to be treated

Many people have a cynical view of the business world. They see dishonesty, a lack of integrity, and unfairness. These do exist. But, if you maintain a sense of fair play it will serve you well. You will earn trust in your business dealings. You will develop lasting business relationships. You will gain the respect of others. Those who play the game in an unfair way may win, but usually they do not last on the playing field.

"Real" Winning

Here I am using the word real to mean genuine. Real winning is about winning in a way that is true to who you are. Winning is not worth it if you have to dishonor your values. Winning should not involve doing things that harm others. Real winning also involves enduring—going for the long haul and planning to succeed over time.

What is Winning for You?

In his book, *The Art of the Deal*, Donald Trump talks about why he does deals. He says that he does not do it for the money. Deals are his art form. That's his fun. So, for Donald we can say winning for him is making deals. It is winning, losing, being brilliant, and making things happen. As you study leadership, it behooves you to define what winning means to you. That way you set a target. Here are some questions to ask yourself.

Why do I want to win?
What do I want to win at? What game am I playing?
Do I have what I need to win?
What is my strategy?

What resources or skills do I need to make it happen?
Am I on my way to winning? Is what I need in place?

What Price Are You Willing to Pay?

As you define what winning is for you, think about what will be required of you to win. If you are Donald Trump, long hours are one requirement. Superb negotiation skills, good branding, knowing his customer base are others. Requirements can impact how you spend your time, where you live, how you live, how you interact with others, your stress level, and who and what you surround yourself with. These are significant impacts and should be carefully considered. What will be demanded of you? Are you willing to do it? Above all, stay true to your values. Winning is never worth negating who you are.

What Will You Do About It?

We've discussed the importance of having a strategy. You will need a strategy to become a winner. Are you willing to do what you need to in order to win? If you want to be chosen as the next Apprentice, are you willing to audition, to market yourself, to quit your job, to compete under pressure, and to risk losing it all? If you want to win, you need commitment and endurance.

Personal and Professional Balance

We are back to balance again. Balance is a significant asset in your quest to win. Balance assures you have the energy you need. Balance brings harmony to your life. Balance is needed to endure. Make sure achieving and maintaining balance is part of your strategy to win.

A Winning Perspective

Never underestimate the importance of attitude. I don't mean ego or false bravado. Adopt a winning perspective and see yourself as the winner you are. Believe in yourself. Show the world that you are a winner.

The Rewards of Winning

I think the biggest rewards of winning are personal ones. You are fulfilled with life, you know you have what it takes, you make yourself and the world better in some way. Ultimately, go for this.

Parting Thoughts

Well, we did it. Together we took a deep look at leadership. I hope my thoughts have made a difference. You may have noticed that my perspective is a personal one. I believe that it is through knowing who you are, honoring yourself, and acknowledging the power you innately have that you can be a leader. It is not about mimicking someone else's way or following another's path. It is about your uniqueness—discovering it and living it.

I hope you will come back to this book as you continue on your path to leadership. Get what you need to support you. Coaching is a wonderful service of motivation, support, and encouragement. You can keep up with what I am doing by accessing my web site: www.MovingForward.net. You can reach me at:

Moving Forward Personal and Professional Coaching
P.O. Box 1372
Littlerock, CA 93543
Phone: 661-944-6329
E-Mail: Ann@MovingForward.net

I would love to hear from you: how your journey of leadership is going, if the book was helpful to you, and any ideas you have to help foster individual leadership. I wish you all the best.

Ann

APPENDIX A
A GUIDE TO VIEWING
THE APPRENTICE AS A CASE STUDY

Viewing *The Apprentice* as a case study is a way you can deepen your learning of the leadership lessons from the show. Case studies are used in schools and organizations to analyze business performance. There are varying formats for case studies. Generally, a case study profiles a business, a particular business situation, the challenges the business faced, the solution found, the results, and the benefits. With a group, or on your own, you can develop a format for a case study of the next season of *The Apprentice*. You can write a case study for each episode of the show, looking at each team's performance. Or, you can write a case study that follows one candidate throughout their time on the show or address performance according to your own criteria. Here are a few ways to view *The Apprentice* as a case study. I am sure you can have fun with this and come up with your own ways as well.

Following Team Performance

This format is episode-based and follows the performance of each team on the assigned task. This case study allows you to analyze performance the way Donald does—by team performance. It begins with a description of the task and what resources and instructions are given to each team, and, it lists the members of the team. As you watch the show you analyze team performance looking at: what issues the team faces, how effectively the team organizes itself, key decisions made and whether they achieve desired result, challenges faced, solutions found, skill and creativity in their approach, team coordination during task, results, and contributing factors to the team's win or loss. Exhibit A presents a form you can use for a team performance case study.

> **EXHIBIT A**
> **Team Performance Case Study**
> (Available for download at www.LeadershipOnTrial.com)
> Task Description:
> Instructions Given:
> Resources Given:
> Project Manager:
> Team Members:
> Issues faced as task begins:
> Effectiveness in organizing team:
> Key decisions made and if they achieved desired result:
>
> Challenges faced and Solutions Found:
> Challenge   Solution
>
>
> Skill and Creativity in Approach to Task:
> Team Coordination During Task:
> Results:
> Contributing Factors to Team's Win/Loss:

Following One Candidate

For this case study, follow one candidate until they are fired or chosen as The Apprentice. This case study gives you the opportunity to look in depth at the candidate's leadership potential. It begins with a profile of the candidate including name, profession, and whatever you know about them as you begin. It then profiles their performance on each task, including skills displayed, strengths, weaknesses, missteps, knowledge base for task, effectiveness of interpersonal relationships, and how they perform in boardroom. As the episodes progress you perform a running SWOT Analysis—strengths, weaknesses, opportunities, and threats involved in their quest to be The Apprentice. Exhibit B presents forms you can use for the individual candidate case study.

EXHIBIT B
Individual Candidate Case Study
Profile/SWOT Page

(Available for download at www.LeadershipOnTrial.com)

Name:
Profession:
What you know about them:
Strengths:
Weaknesses:
Opportunities:
Threats:

EXHIBIT B-1
Individual Candidate Case Study
Task Performance Page

(Available for download at www.LeadershipOnTrial.com)

Task Description:
Fellow Team Members:
Skills Displayed:
Strengths:
Weaknesses:
Missteps:
Knowledge Base for Task:
Effectiveness of Interpersonal Relationships:
Performance in Boardroom:

A Case Study from Donald's Point of View

For this case study, put yourself in Donald's place. You will analyze the candidates' performance on each task and make a case for who you think should be fired. Develop your own criteria for choosing an apprentice, and follow along with candidate performance on the show. Determine which candidate you would pick and why. Compare your choice to Donald's. Exhibit C suggests a format you can use or tailor to your needs.

EXHIBIT C
You Choose Case Study
(one form per task)
(Available for download at www.LeadershipOnTrial.com)

My Criteria for Choosing The Apprentice:
(Note: Develop your own criteria or as done here, use the seven leadership lessons)
Take Risks:
Be Yourself:
Know the Game:
Maintain Balance:
Have a Strategy:
Think Outside the Box:
Know When to Join and When to Lead:

EXHIBIT C-1
You Choose Case Study
(one form per task)
(Available for download at www.LeadershipOnTrial.com)
Candidates Names:
Using your criteria determine:
Best Performer:
Why:
Worst Performer:
Why:
Noteworthy performances by other candidates:
Poor performance by other candidates:
Who should be fired:

APPENDIX B
LEADERSHIP RESOURCES

LEADERSHIP

Books
Synchronicity: The Inner Path of Leadership, Joseph Jaworski, Berrett-Koehler Publishers (1996)

Leadership and the New Science, Margaret J. Wheatley, Berrett-Koehler Publishers (1992/4)

Harvard Business Review on Leadership (Harvard Business Review Series) by Henry Mintzberg, Harvard Business School Press (1998)

Business Leadership, by James M. Kouzes Jossey-Bass (2003)

Ethics, the Heart of Leadership, by Joanne B. Ciulla (Editor), Praeger Paperback (1998)

The Leadership Pipeline, by Ram Charan, Jossey-Bas (2000)

The One Minute Manager, by Ken Blanchard & Spencer Johnson, William Morrow (1982)

On Becoming a Leader: The Leadership Classic, Updated And Expanded by Warren Bennis, Perseus Publishing; Rev edition (April 2003)

Play Like a Man, Win Like a Woman, by Gail Evans: Former Executive VP of CNN, Broadway Books; (September 2001)

The Power of Full Engagement: Managing Energy, Not Time, is the Key to High Performance and Personal Renewal, by Jim Loehr, Free Press; (February 2003), (Paperback Jan 2005)

Institutes
Athena Foundation, www.athenafoundation.org

National Hispanic Leadership Institute, www.nhli.org

Asian Pacific American Women's Leadership Institute, www.apawli.org

United States Hispanic Leadership Institute, www.ushli.com

African American Leadership Institute, www.academy.umd.edu.scholarship/aali/

Executive Leadership Institute (public and community service), www.eli.pdx.edu

Center for Leadership Development, Dialogue, and Inquiry, New York University, Wagner Graduate School of Public Service, www.nyu.edu.wagner

Asian Leadership Institute, www.asianleadership.com

The Aspen Institute, www.aspeninstitute.org

Magazines

The Leadership & Organization Development Journal, Strategy and Leadership Magazine

Harvard Business Review

Leadership Magazine

Academy of Strategic and Organizational Leadership Journal

Executive Leadership Magazine

The Leadership Quarterly

Journal of Leadership and Organization Studies

GETTING COMFORTABLE WITH RISK

Books

Making Enterprise Risk Management Pay Off: How Leading Companies Implement Risk Management, by Thomas L. Barton, William G. Shenkir, Paul L. Walker Pearson Education; 1st edition (February 2002)

Transitions: Making Sense of Life's Changes, William Bridges, Addison Wesley Publishing Company (1980)

Right Risk: 10 Powerful Principles for Taking Giant Leaps with Your Life, by Bill Treasurer, Berrett-Koehler Publishers; (May 2003)

Skunk Works : A Personal Memoir of My Years of Lockheed, by Leo Janos, Ben R. Rich : Back Bay Books; (February 1996)

Changing Directions Without Losing your Way, Paul and Sarah Edwards, Tarcher Putnam (2001)

Team Secrets of the Navy Seals, by Robert Needham Publisher: Andrews McMeel Publishing; (May 2003)

Fearless Living: Live Without Excuses and Love Without Regret, by Rhonda Britten, Perigee Books (April 2002)

Fight Your Fear and Win: 7 Skills for Performing Your Best Under Pressure--At Work, in Sports, on Stage, by Dr. Don Greene, Broadway Books (February 2002)

Feel the Fear and Do It Anyway, by Susan Jeffers, Publisher: Ballantine Books; Reissue edition (May 1988)

Touch the Top of the World: A Blind Man's Journey to Climb Farther Than the Eye Can See, by Erik Weihenmayer, Plume Books; Reissue edition (March 2002)

To Reach the Clouds: My High Wire Walk Between the Twin Towers, by Philippe Petit, Publisher: North Point Press; 1st edition (September 2002)

Losing My Virginity: How I've Survived, Had Fun, and Made a Fortune Doing Business My Way, by Richard Branson, Three Rivers Press; 1st U.S. P edition (October 1999)

Swimming to Antarctica: Tales of a Long-Distance Swimmer, by Lynne Cox, Knopf; 1st edition (January 2004)

Web Sites
Outward Bound USA, www.outwardbound.org
Dale Carnegie Training, www.dalecarnegie.com
Toastmasters International, www.toastmasters.org

CREATIVITY AND INNOVATION

Books
The Artist's Way, by Julia Cameron, Jeremy P. Tarcher; 10th Anniversary Edition (2002)
The Artist's Way at Work, by Mark Bryan, Julia Cameron, and Catherine Allen, William Morrow (1998)
The Heart Aroused, Poetry and the Preservation of the Soul in Corporate America, by David Whyte, Currency Doubleday (1994)
Creativity in Business, by Michael Ray, Main Street Books (Reissue edition 1988)
Thinkertoys (A Handbook of Business Creativity), by Michael Michalko, Ten Speed Press (1991)
The Big Book of Business Games: Icebreakers, Creativity Exercises and Meeting Energizers, by John W. Newstrom, Edward E. Scannell, McGraw-Hill (1995)
The Creative Priority: Putting Innovation to Work in Your Business, by Jerry Hirshberg, Harper Business (1999)
The Power of Strategy Innovation: A New Way of Linking Creativity and Strategic Planning to Discover Great Business Opportunities, by Robert E. Johnston, AMACOM (2003)
Creativity Inc.: Building an Inventive Organization, by Jeff Mauzy, Harvard Business School Press (2003)
Training to Imagine: Practical Improvisational Theatre Techniques to Enhance Creativity, Teamwork, Leadership, and Learning, by Kat Koppett, Stylus Publishing, LLC (2001)
Creativity at Work, by Jeff DeGraff, Jossey-Bass (2002)

Cards and Games
Creative Whack Pack, by Roger von Oech, available at Amazon.com
Cranium Board Game, available at Amazon.com and Retail Stores
KnowBrainer Card Deck, www.solutionpeople.com/kbtool.htm
Think Pack: Brainstorming Cards, by Michael Micalko available at Amazon.com

Magazines

Fast Company, www.FastCompany.com

Brain Power Magazine, www.msoworld.com/brain/mag/index.html

Organizations

Center for Creative Leadership, www.ccl.org

American Creativity Association, www.amcreativityassoc.org

The Creative Education Foundation, www.creativeeducationfoundation.org

Web Sites

The Gurteen Knowledge Website, www.gurteen.com

Means Business, a unique concept database of 20,000 key ideas from business and management books, www.meansbusiness.com

Creativity Portal promotes the exploration and expression of personal creativity through free learning, arts, crafts, writings, and other creative activities. Site has how-to resources, inspiring articles, downloadable projects, fun and humor, and motivation to be creative. www.creativity-portal.com

Creativity and Innovation www.MyCoted.com

PROFESSIONAL DEVELOPMENT/FULFILLMENT

Books

Finding Your Own North Star, by Martha Beck, Three Rivers Press (2001)

Now What? 90 Days to a New Life Direction, by Laura Berman Fortgang, Tarcher Penquin (2004)

The Art of Schmooze, by Beth Mende Conny, Blue Island Press (2004)

Take Yourself to the Top, by Laura Berman Fortgang, Warner Books (1998)

Games Mother Never Taught You, Betty Lehan Harragan, by Warner Books (1978)

Nice Girls Don't Get the Corner Office, by Lois P. Frankel, Warner Books (2004)

Newsletters

BoomerCareer.com is a publication for sophisticated, active Baby Boomers who want their careers to be vital components in fulfilled and challenging lives. www.boomercareer.com

BALANCE

Books

Take Time for Your Life, by Cheryl Richardson, Broadway Books (1998)

Love and Power, by Lynn Andrews, Harper Collins (1997)

The 9 Steps to Financial Freedom, by Suze Orman, Three Rivers Press (1997/2000)

The Energy of Money, by Maria Nemeth, Ballantine Wellspring (1997)

Real Prosperity: Using the Power of Intuition to Create Financial and Spiritual Abundance, by Lynn Robinson, Andrews McMeel Publishing; (September 2004)

Booklets
Achieving Balance in Your Life, by Ann Vanino, available at www.MovingForward.net or by calling (US) 661-944-6329

Columns/Newsletters
Coaching Corner, by Ann Vanino, available by subscription, at www.MovingForward.net or by calling (US) 661-944-6329

Life Makeover Newsletter, www.cherylrichardson.com

Magazines
O Magazine (Oprah)
Real Simple Magazine
Spirituality & Health Magazine
Self Magazine

Television
Oxygen Channel
Lifetime Channel
Wisdom TV

STAYING ORGANIZED

Books
The Organized Executive: The Classic Program for Productivity: New Ways to Manage Time Paper, People, and the Digital Office, by Stephanie Winston, Warner Business Books (February 2001)

The Organizing Sourcebook: Nine Strategies for Simplifying Your Life, by Kathy Waddill, McGraw-Hill (July 2001)

K-I-S-S Guide to Organizing Your Life, by Dr. Donald Wetmore DK Publishing (2001)

Organizing from the Inside Out, by Julie Morgenstern, Owl Books; 2nd Rev&Up edition (September 2004)

Video
Organizing from the Inside Out with Julie Morgenstern, Video: PBS Home Video (2000)

Web Sites

National Association of Professional Organizers, www.napo.net

The Paper Tiger, www.ThePaperTiger.com (Paper Filing System)

FileSolutions, www.filesolutions.com

Organize Your Office, Attractive, customizable shelving & organizers perfect for offices. www.SmartFurniture.com

Stacks and Stacks, www.stacksandstacks.com

Retail Stores

Organized Living, www.organizedliving.com
Hold Everything, www.holdeverything.com
The Container Store, www.containerstore.com

ABOUT THE AUTHOR

Ann Vanino is a well-known personal and professional coach, writer, and speaker and the founder of Moving Forward Personal and Professional Coaching. Moving Forward is dedicated to helping clients create the life they want and helping business owners and executives build successful, prosperous, and well-managed organizations. Ann has coached clients through job-related issues since 1996. She has worked with hundreds of people, helping them empower themselves and their organizations to achieve success. Her work touches countless others through seminars, speaking engagements, publications, and classes. Ann writes a weekly newspaper column, Coaching Corner, that guides readers to a fulfilling life.

Ann's business career spans over twenty years, including management positions at the U. S. Environmental Protection Agency and as Assistant Commissioner of New York City's Hazardous Materials Emergency Response Team, overseeing its response to over six hundred chemical emergencies a year. The team was a national leader in emergency response in the 1980s. In this role, Ann interacted with a wide range of professionals, including police, fire and health officials, media representatives, responders from local "haz mat" teams, state and federal government officials, business owners, and corporate representatives. Since 1988, Ann has worked in the private sector. As a consultant and business owner, she helped Fortune 500 corporations and government agencies comply with government regulations and manage their environmental programs effectively. In 1997, Ann entered the coaching profession full time. Ann was born and raised in New York City. She received a Master's Degree from New York University's Wagner School of Public Service and a Bachelor's Degree from The State University of New York at Albany.

You can learn more about Ann and coaching on her web site: www.MovingForward.net or www.LeadershipOnTrial.com.

Ways To Continue the Learning with Ann

Subscribe to Ann's Coaching Corner Weekly Column
Would you like to have motivation, support, and encouragement from a coach on a weekly basis? Are you ready to learn new ways to approach your work, your life, and your relationships? Each column addresses an aspect of life, work, or relationships and contains an inspiring quote, Ann's insights, questions to ask yourself, and an exercise to take action. Reading Coaching Corner each week will give you the tools to move forward to the life you desire.

One-On-One Coaching
One-on-one coaching is all about you! Work with Ann to achieve the results you seek. Begin with an initial session, in person or by phone, to get to know each other, to identify your values, and to identify your vision of a fulfilling life. Together, identify the steps you want to take to change your life, "design the alliance" for our coaching and then get in action!

Group Coaching
Join Ann in a group adventure designed to help you achieve the results you seek. Group coaching is a supportive environment that uses coaching techniques and group interaction to assist participants in moving forward in their life. Each group coaches for three months.

Full Court Press
Full Court Press is a short-term, focused coaching program designed by you and Moving Forward to meet a specific goal in a defined period of time. Full Court Press can be employed for any goal. You can use this service to meet all your needs!

Business Coaching
Ann works with large and small organizations to: design effective infrastructures; prepare for and manage growth; optimize organizational structure for efficient and effective performance; create an environment of teamwork and employee satisfaction within the organization; assess organizational needs; develop short and long term strategic plans, and develop leadership within the organization. This service is designed specifically to meet your organization's needs and can include: one-on-one executive coaching, one-on-one employee coaching, organizational assessments, strategic plan development, and special projects.

For more information visit Ann's web site, www.MovingForward.net or call her at 661-944-6329